J O N L _ _

BRITISH THEATRE.

VOL. VI.

CONTAINING,

I:

THE MAN OF THE WORLD.

II.

THE TRUE BORN IRISHMAN.

III.

LOVE A LA MODE.

IV.

THE GOVERNESS.

D U B L I N:

PRINTED BY JOHN CHAMBERS,

FOR WILLIAM JONES, No. 86, DAME-STREET.

1795.

THE

MAN OF THE WORLD:

A

COMEDY.

BY CHARLES MACKLIN, ESQ.

ADAPTED FOR

THEATRICAL REPRESENTATION.

AS PERFORMED AT THE

THEATRES-ROYAL,

**DRURY-LANE, COVENT-GARDEN, AND
SMOCK-ALLEY.**

REGULATED FROM THE PROMPT-BOOKS,

By Permission of the Managers.

" The Lines distinguished by inverted Commas, are omitted in the Representation."

DUBLIN:

PRINTED BY GRAISBERRY AND CAMPBELL,
FOR WILLIAM JONES, NO. 86, DAME-STREET.

M DCC XCIII.

SMOCK-ALLEY.

Men.

SIR PERTINAX MAC SYCOPHANT,	Mr. Macklin.
EGERTON,	Mr. M'Cready.
LORD LUMBERCOURT,	Mr. Mofs.
SIDNEY,	Mr. Swindal.
MELVILLE	Mr. Fotteral.
COUNSELLOR PLAUSIBLE,	Mr. G. Dawfon.
SERJEANT EITHERSIDE,	Mr. Glenville.
SAM,	Mr. Lynch.
JOHN,	Mr. Malone.
TOMLINS,	Mr. Smith.

Women.

LADY MAC SYCOPHANT,	Mrs. Sparks.
LADY RODOLPHA LUMBERCOURT,	Mrs. Egerton.
CONSTANTIA,	Mifs Jarrett.
BETTY HINT,	Mrs. Cornelys.
NANNY,	Mrs. O'Neill.

SCENE, Sir Pertinax Mac Sycophant's Houfe in the Country.

TIME—Three Hours.

MAN OF THE WORLD.

ACT I. SCENE I.

A Library in Sir PERTINAX'S *Houſe.*

Enter BETTY *and* FOOTMAN.

Betty.

THE poſtman is at the gate, Sam, pray ſtep and take in the letters.

Sam. John, the gardener is gone for them, Mrs. Betty.

Bet. Bid John bring them to me, Sam, tell him I'm here in the library.

Sam. I will ſend him to your ladyſhip, in a crack.

[*Exit Sam.*

Enter NANNY.

Nan. Miſs Conſtantia deſires to ſpeak to you, Mrs. Betty.

Bet. How is ſhe now, Nanny, any better?

Nan. Something, but very low spirited still, I verily believe it is as you say.

Bet. Nay, I would take my book oath of it.—I cannot be deceived in that point, Nanny—ay, ay; her business is done; she is certainly breeding, depend upon it.

Nan. Why, so the house-keeper thinks too.

Bet. Nay, I know the father! the very man that ruined her!

Nan. The deuce you do!

Bet. As sure as you are alive, Nanny, or I am greatly deceived, and yet I can't be deceived neither—Was not that the cook that came gallopping so hard over the common just now?

Nan. The same. How very hard he gallopped. He has been but three quarters of an hour, he says, coming from Hyde Park corner.

Bet. And, what time will the family be down?

Nan. He has orders to have dinner ready by five; there are to be lawyers, and a great deal of company. —He fancies there is to be a private wedding here to-night, between our young master Charles, and lord Lumbercourt's daughter—the Scotch lady:—who, he says, is just come from Bath on purpose to be married to him.

Bet. Ay, ay, lady Rodolpha, as they call her, nay, like enough: for I know it has been talked of a good while; well, go tell Miss Constantia that I will be with her immediately.

Nan. I shall, Mrs. Betty.   [*Exit Nanny.*

Bet. So! I find they all believe the impertinent

creature is breeding, that is pure, it will foon reach
my lady's ear, I warrant.

Enter JOHN, *with letters.*

Well, John, ever a letter for me ?

John. No, Mrs. Betty, but here's one for Mifs
Conftantia.

Bet. Give it me—hem—my lady's hand.

John. And here is one which the poftman fays is
for my young mafter, but it is a ftrange direction
[*reads.*] To Charles Egerton, efq.

Bet. O ! yes—yes—that is for mafter Charles,
John, for he has dropt his father's name of Mac Sy-
cophant, and has taken up that of Egerton.—The
Parliament has ordered it.

John. The parliament ! pry'thee why fo, Mrs.
Betty ?

Bet. Why, you muft know, John, that my lady,
his mother, was an Egerton by her father ; fhe ftole
a match with our old mafter, for which all her fa-
mily, on both fides have hated fir Pertinax, and the
whole crew of the Mac Sycophants ever fince.

John. Except mafter Charles, Mrs. Betty.

Bet. O ! they doat upon him, for tho' he be a
Mac Sycophant, he's the pride of all my lady's fa-
mily.—And fo, John, my lady's uncle, fir Stanley
Egerton, dying an old batchelor, and, as I faid before,
mortally hating our old mafter, and the whole crew of
the Mac Sycophants, left his whole eftate to mafter
Charles, who was his god-fon ; but on condition tho',
that he fhou'd drop his father's name of Mac Syco-

phant, and take up that of Egerton, and that is the
reafon, John, why the parliament has made him
change his name.

John. I am glad that mafter Charles has got the
eftate however, for he is a fweet tempered gentleman.

Bet. As ever lived, but come, John, as I know
you love Mifs Conftantia, and are fond of an oppor-
tunity of fpeaking to her, I will make you happy, you
fhall carry her letter to her.

John. Shall I, Mrs. Betty ? I am very much oblig-
ed to you, where is fhe ?

Bet. In the houfekeeper's room, fettling the de-
fert.—Give me Mr. Egerton's letter, I will lay it on
the table in his drefling room, I fee its from his bro-
ther, Mr. Sandy ; fo, now go and deliver your letter
to your fweetheart, John.

John. That I will, Mrs. Betty, and I am much
obliged to you for the favour of letting me carry it to
her ; for tho' fhe fhould never have me, yet I fhall
always love her, and wifh to be near her, fhe is fo
fweet a creature—Your fervant, Mrs. Betty, I will
kifs the letter for her fake—fweet, fweet, dear Mifs
Conftantia !—O ! if I was but kifling her hand,
Betty, now, inftead of this letter, how happy fhou'd
I be—Your fervant, Mrs. Betty.   [*Exit John.*

Bet. Your fervant, John—ha ! ha ! ha ! poor fel-
low, he perfectly doats on her, and daily follows her
about with nofegays and fruit, and the firft of every
thing in the feafon ; ay, and my young mafter Charles
too, he is in as bad a way as the gardener—in fhort,
every body loves her, and that is one reafon why I
hate her :—for my part, I wonder what the deuce the

men see in her—a creature that was taken in for
charity—I am sure she is not so handsome — I wish she
was out of the family once, if she was, I might then
stand a chance of being my lady's favourite myself;
ay, and perhaps of getting one of my young masters
for a sweetheart—or at least, the chaplain—but as to
him, there would be no such great catch, if I should
get him—I will try for him however; and my first
step shall be, to let the doctor know all I have disco-
vered about Constantia's intrigues with her spark at
Hadley—Yes, that will do, for the doctor loves to
talk with me, and always smiles and jokes with me
[*laughs*] he, he,—he loves to hear me talk too, and I
verily believe he, he, he, that he has a sneaking kind-
ness for me! besides, this story will make him have a
good opinion of my honesty, and that I am sure will
be one step towards it.—O bless me I here he comes,
and my young master with him—I'll watch an oppor-
tunity to speak to him, as soon as he is alone, for I
will blow her up, I am resolved, as great a favourite,
and as cunning as she is.   [*Exit.*

Enter EGERTON *(in great warmth and emotion)*
SIDNEY *following, as in earnest conversation.*

Sid Nay, dear Charles, but why are you so impe-
tuous! Why do you break from me so abruptly?

Egert. I have done, sir—You have refused—I
have nothing more to say upon the subject—I am sa-
tisfied.

Sid. [*Spoke with a glow of tender friendship.*] Come,

B

come, correct this warmth ; it is the only weak ingredient in your nature ; and you ought to watch it carefully ; if I am wrong, I will submit without reserve ; but confider the nature of your requeft, and how it would affect me. From your earlieft youth your father has honoured me with the care of your education, and the general conduct of your mind ; and however fingular and morofe his behaviour may be towards others, to me he has ever been refpectful and liberal. I am now under his roof too—and becaufe I will not abet an unwarrantable paffion, by an abufe of my facred character, in marrying you beneath your rank, and in direct oppofition to your father's hopes and happinefs —you blame—you angrily break from me, and call me unkind.

Egert. [*With kindnefs and conviction.*] Dear Sidney, for my warmth I ftand condemned ; but for my marriage with Conftantia, I think I can juftify it upon every principle of filial duty, honour and worldly prudence.

Sid. Only make that appear, Charles, and you know you may command me.

Egert. I am fenfible how unworthy it appears in a fon to defcant on the unamiable paffions of a father ; but as we are alone, and friends, I cannot help obferving, in my own defence, that when a father will not allow the ufe of reafon to any of his family— when his purfuit of greatnefs makes him a flave abroad—only to be a tyrant at home—when his narrow partiality to Scotland, on every trivial occafion, provokes him to enmity even with his wife and children, only becaufe they dare give a national preference where they think it is moft juftly due—and when merely to gratify his own ambition, he would marry his son into a family he detests. [*With great warmth*]. Sure, Sidney, a son thus circumstanced (from the dignity of human nature, and the feelings of a loving heart) has a right, not only to protest against the blindness of the parent, but to pursue those measures, that virtue and happiness point out.

Sid. The violent temper of Sir Pertinax, I own, cannot on many occasions be defended—but still your intended alliance with Lord Lumbercourt.——

Egert. O! contemptible! A trifling, quaint, haughty, voluptuous! servile too!—the mere lackey of party and corruption ; who for the prostitution of near thirty years, and the ruin of a noble fortune, has had the despicable satisfaction, and the infamous honour, of being kicked up, and kicked down, kicked in, and kicked out—just as the insolence, compassion, or conveniency of leaders predominated ; and now, being forsaken by all parties, his whole political consequence amounts to, the power of franking a letter, and the right honourable privilege of not paying a tradesman's bill.

Sid. Well, but, dear Charles, you are not to wed my lord, but his daughter.

Egert. Who is as disagreeable for a companion, as her father is for a friend or an ally.

Sid. Ha! ha! ha! What, her Scotch accent, I suppose, offends you?

Egert. No—upon my honour—not in the least, I think it entertaining in her, but were it otherwise, in decency—and, indeed, in national affection (being a Scotchman myself) I can have no objection to her on *that account—besides,* she is my near relation.

Sid. So I underſtand, but how comes Lady Rodol-
pha, who, I find, was born in England, to be bred in
Scotland ?

Egert. From the dotage of an old, formal, obſti-
nate, ſtiff, rich, Scotch Grandmother ; who, upon a
promiſe of leaving this grandchild all her fortune,
which is very conſiderable, wou'd have the girl ſent
to her to Scotland, when ſhe was but a year old ; and
there has ſhe been bred up ever ſince, with this old
lady, in all the vanity, and unlimited indulgence,
that fondneſs and admiration could beſtow on a ſpoil-
ed child, a fancied beauty ! and a pretended wit !

Sid. O ! you are too ſevere on her.

Egert. I do not think ſo, Sidney ; for ſhe ſeems a
being expreſsly faſhioned by nature, to figure in theſe
days of levity and diſſipation ! her ſpirits are inex-
hauſtible ! her parts ſtrong and lively ! with a ſaga-
city that diſcerns, and a talent not unhappy in paint-
ing the weak ſide of whatever comes before her.——
But what raiſes her merit to the higheſt pitch, in the
laughing world is, her boundleſs vanity, in the ex-
ertion of thoſe talents, which often renders herſelf
much more ridiculous, than the moſt whimſical of
the characters ſhe expoſes.——And is this a woman fit
to make my happineſs ? This the partner that Sidney
would recommend to me for life ? To you, who beſt
know me, I appeal.

Sid. Why, Charles, it is a delicate point—unfit
for me to determine—beſides your father has ſet his
mind upon the match.

Egert. [*Impatiently.*] All that I know—but ſtill I
aſk, and inſiſt upon your candid judgment, is ſhe the

kind of woman that you think cou'd poffibly contribute to my happinefs ?—I beg you will give me an explicit. anfwer.

Sid. The fubject is difagreeable—But fince I muft. fpeak—I do not think fhe is.

Egert. I know you do not ; and I am fure you never will advife the match.

Sid. I never did—I never will.

Egert. [*With a ftart of joy.*] You make me happy— which, I affure you, I never could be with your judgment againft me on this point.

Sid. And yet, Charles, give me leave to obferve, that Lady Rodolpha, with all her ridiculous laughing vanity, has a goodnefs of heart, and a kind of vivacity, that not only entertains, but upon feeing her two or three times, improves upon you, and when her torrent of fpirits abates, and fhe condefcends to converfe gravely, you will really like her.

Egert. Why, aye, fhe is fprightly, good-humoured, and tho' whimfical, and often too high in her colouring of characters, and in the trifling bufinefs of the idle world, yet I think fhe has principles and a good heart ; but in a partner for life, Sidney, (you know your own precept—your own judgment) affection, capricious in its nature, muft have fomething even in the external manners—nay, in the very mode, not only of beauty, but virtue itfelf, which both heart and judgment muft approve, or our happinefs in that delicate point cannot be lafting.

Sid. I grant it.

Egert. And that mode, that amiable effential, I never can meet with but in Conftantia.—You figh.

Sid. No, I only wifh that Conftantia had a fortune equal to yours; but pray, Charles, fuppofe I had been fo indifcreet as to have agreed to marry you to Conftantia, would fhe have confented, think you?

Egert. That I cannot fay pofitively: but I fuppofe fo.

Sid. Did you never fpeak to her, upon that fubject then?

Egert. In general terms only; never directly afked her confent in form; but I will this very moment, for I have no afylum from my father's arbitrary defign, but my Conftantia's arms—Pray do not ftir from hence—I will return inftantly; I know fhe will fubmit to your advice, and I am fure you will perfuade her to my wifh, as my life, my peace, my earthly happinefs depend upon my Conftantia.

[*Exit.*

Sid. Poor Charles! He little dreams that I love Conftantia—but to what degree I knew not myfelf, till he importuned me to join their hands.—Yes, I love, but muft not be a rival—for he is dear to me as fraternal friendfhip—my benefactor, my friend, and that name is facred. It is our better felf, and ought to be preferred.—For the man who gratifies his paffions at the expence of his friend's happinefs, wants but a head to contrive, for he has a heart capable of the blackeft vice.

Enter BETTY, *running up to him.*

Bet. I beg pardon, fir, for my intrufion; I hope, fir, I do not difturb you.

Sid. Not in the leaft, Mrs. Betty.

Bet. I humbly hope you will excufe me, fir,—but I wanted to break my mind to your honour—about a fcruple—that lies upon my confcience—and, indeed, I fhou'd not have prefumed to trouble you, fir, but that I know you are my young mafter's friend—and, indeed, a friend to the whole family—[*runs up to him and curtfeys very low.*] for to give you your due, fir, you are as good a preacher as ever went into a pulpit.

Sid. Ha! ha! ha! Do you think fo, Mrs. Betty?

Bet. Ay in truth do I—and as good a gentleman too as ever came into a family, and one that never gives a fervant a hard word; nor that does any one an ill turn, neither behind one's back, nor before one's face.

Sid. Ha! ha! ha!—why you are a mighty well fpoken woman, Mrs. Betty, and I am extremely beholden to you for your good character of me.

Bet. Indeed, fir, it is no more than what you deferve; and what all the fervants fay of you.

Sid. I am much obliged to them, Mrs. Betty— But pray, what are your commands with me?

Bet. Why, I will tell you, fir,—to be fure, I am but a fervant, as a body may fay, and every tub fhould ftand upon its own bottom; but [*fhe holds him familiarly, looks about cautioufly, and fpeaks in a low familiar tone of great fecrecy.*] my young mafter is now in the china room, in clofe conference with Mifs Conftantia—I know what they are about—but that

is no bufinefs of mine—and therefore I made bold
to liften a little ; becaufe you know, fir, one would
be fure, before one took away any body's good
name.

Sid. Very true, Mrs. Betty—very true, indeed.

Bet. Oh ! heavens forbid that I fhould take away
any young woman's good name, unlefs I had good
reafon for it :—But, fir, if I am in this place alive—
as I liftened with my ear clofe to the door—I heard
my young mafter afk Mifs Conftantia—the plain mar-
riage queftion ; upon which, I ftarted and trembled—
nay, my very confcience ftirred within me fo, that I,
I, I cou'd not help peeping thro' the key-hole.

Sid. Ha ! ha ! ha !—And fo your confcience made
you peep thro' the key-hole, Mrs. Betty ?—Ha !

Bet. It did indeed, fir, and then I faw my young
mafter down upon his knees ; and what do you think
he was doing ?—Lord blefs us !—kiffing her hand,
as if he would eat it ; and protefting and affuring her,
he knew that you, fir, would confent to the match
—and then, O ! my good fir, the tears ran down her
cheeks as faft——

Sid. Ay !

Bet. [*Crying tenderly*] They did indeed, fir ; I
wou'd not tell your reverence a lie for the world.

Sid. I believe it, Mrs. Betty, I believe it ; and
what did Conftantia fay to all this ?

Bet. [*Sneering feverely, and fhaking her head.*] O !
fhe is fly enough—fhe looks as if butter would not
melt in her mouth, but all is not gold that gliftens—
fmooth water you know runs deepeft, [*fpeaks this with*

forrow] I am forry my young mafter makes himfelf fuch a fool, very forry, indeed; but um—ha—take my word for it, he is not the man, [*fneeringly.*] for tho' fhe looks as modeft as a maid at a chriftening. [*hefitating.*] Yet, a—when fweethearts meet in the dufk of the evening—and ftay together a whole hour in a dark grove—and—a—embrace—and kifs—and weep at parting—why then you know, fir—it is eafy to guefs althe. reft.

Sid. Why, did Conftantia meet any body in this manner?

Bet. [*Starting with furprife.*] O, Heavens! I beg, fir, you will not mifapprehend me! for I affure you I do not believe they did any harm—that is—not in the grove—at leaft not when I was there—and fhe may be honeftly married for aught I know —O lud! Sir, I would not fay an ill thing of Mifs Conftantia for all the world—for to befure fhe is a good creature—'tis true my lady took her in for charity – and, indeed, has bred her up to the mufic, and figures – ay, and to reading all the books about Homer—and Paradife—and gods and devils—and every thing in the world—as if fhe had been a duchefs;—but fome people are born with luck in their mouths—and then—as the faying is, you may throw them into the fea—[*deports herfelf moft affectedly.*] but if I had had dancing mafters, and mufic, and French monfieurs to teach me, fmiles, coquets, and puts on important airs of affectation, I believe I might read the globes, and the maps, and have danced, and have been as clever as other folks.   B 3

Sid. Ha! ha! ha!—No doubt of it, Mrs. Betty, no doubt in the leaft. But, Mrs. Betty, you mentioned fomething of a dark walk—about kiffing—a fweetheart—and Conftantia.

Bet. O lud! Sir, I don't know any thing of the matter—fhe may be very honeft for ought I know—I only fay, that they did meet in the dark walk ; and all the fervants are laughing and tittering, and conftantly obferving, that Mifs Conftantia wears her ftays very loofe—looks very pale—is fick in a morning, and after dinner ;—and as fure as my name is Betty Hint, fomething has happened that 1 won't name ;- but nine months hence, a certain perfon in this family, may afk me to ftand godmother, for I think I know what's what, when I fee it, as well as another.

Sid. No doubt you do, Mrs Betty.

Bet. I do, indeed, fir, and [*he cries, turns up her eyes, and acts a moft friendly devout hypocrify.*] I am very forry for Mifs Conftantia, I never thought fhe would have taken fuch courfes—for in truth, I love her as if fhe were my own fifter—and tho' all the fervants fay fhe is breeding, yet, for my part, I don't believe it—but one muft fpeak according to one's confcience you know, fir.

Sid. I fee you do, Mrs. Betty.

Bet. I do indeed, fir, and fo your fervant, fir—[*Going away and returning.*] But I hope your worfhip will not mention my name in this bufinefs, or that you had any item from me.

Sid. I fhall not, Mrs. Betty.

Bet. For indeed, fir, I am no bufy-body—nor do I love fending and proving—and I affure you, fir, I hate all tittling and tattling, and goffiping, and back-biting, and taking away a young perfon's character, be her ever fo bad.

Sid. I obferve you do, Mrs. Betty.

Bet. I do indeed, fir, I am the fartheft from it in the world.

Sid. I dare fay you are.

Bet. I am indeed, fir, and fo your humble fer-vant.

Sid. Your fervant, Mrs. Betty.

Bet. [*Afide in great exultation.*] So ! I fee he be-lieves every word I fay—that's charming—I will do her bufinefs for her, I am refolved.   [*Exit.*

Sid. What can this ridiculous creature mean—by her dark walk—her private fpark—her kiffing—and all her flanderous infinuations againft Conftantia, whofe conduct is as unblameable as innocence itfelf? I fee envy is as malignant in a paltry waiting wench, as in the vaineft or moft ambitious lady of the court. It is always a moft infallible mark of the bafeft nature, and merit in the loweft, as in the higheft ftation, muft feel the fhafts of Envy's conftant agents, Falfehood and Slander.

Enter SAM.

Sam. Sir, Mr. Egerton and Mifs Conftantia, de-fire to fpeak with you in the china room.

Sid. Very well, Sam.   [*Exit* Sam.

I will not fee them—What is to be done ? Inform

his father of his intended marriage.—No; that muft not be—for the overbearing temper, and ambitious policy of Sir Pertinax, would exceed all bounds of moderation. He has banifhed one fon already, only for daring to differ from his judgment concerning the merits of Scotch and Englifh hiftorians. But this young man muft not marry Conftantia—wou'd his mother were here : fhe, I fuppofe, knows nothing of his indifcretion, but fhe fhall the moment fhe comes hither—I know it will offend him—no matter, it is our duty to offend, when the offence faves the man we love from a precipitate action, which the world muft condemn, and his own heart, perhaps, upon reflection, for ever repent. Yes, I muft. difcharge the duty of my function, and a friend, tho' I am fure to lofe the man whom I intend to ferve.

[*Exit.*

ACT II. SCENE I.

Enter EGERTON *and* CONSTANTIA.

Conftantia.

MR. Sidney is not here, fir.

Egert. I affure you I left him here, and begged that he wou'd ftay till I returned.

Conſt. His prudence, you ſee, ſir, has made him retire, therefore we had better defer the ſubject till he is preſent. In the mean time, ſir, I hope you will permit me to mention an affair, that has greatly alarmed and perplexed me ; I ſuppoſe you gueſs what it is ?

Egert. I do not upon my word.

Conſt. That's a little ſtrange. You know, ſir, that you and Mr. Sidney did me the honour of breakfaſting with me this morning in my little ſtudy.

Egert. We had that happineſs, madam.

Conſt. Juſt after you left me, opening my book of accounts, which lay in the drawer of the reading deſk, to my great ſurpriſe, I there found this caſe of jewels, containing a moſt elegant pair of ear-rings, and a neck-lace of great value, and two bank bills in this pocket-book, the myſtery of which, I preſume, ſir, you can explain.

Egert. I can.

Conſt. They are of your conveying, then.

Egert. They were, madam.

Conſt I aſſure you they ſtartled and alarmed me.

Egert. I hope it was a kind alarm ; ſuch as bluſhing Virtue feels, when with her hand, ſhe gives her heart and laſt conſent.

Conſt. It was not, indeed, ſir.

Egert. Do not ſay ſo, Conſtantia—come, be kind at once ; my peace and worldly bliſs depend upon this moment.

Conſt. What wou'd you have me do ?

Egert. What love and virtue dictate.

Conft. O! fir, experience but too feverely prove
that fuch unequal matches as ours, never produce
aught but contempt and anger in parents, cenfure
from the world, and a long train of forrow and repen-
tance in the wretched parties, which is but too often
entailed upon their haplefs iffue.

Egert. But that, Conftantia, cannot be our condi-
tion, for my fortune is independent and ample, equal
to luxury and fplendid folly ; I have a right to choofe
the partner of my heart.

Conft. But I have not, fir—I am a dependant on
my lady—a poor, forfaken, helplefs orphan, your
benevolent mother found me ; took me to her bofom,
and there fupplied my parental lofs, with every ten-
der care, indulgent dalliance, and with all the fweet
perfuafion that maternal fondnefs, religious precepts,
polifhed manners, and hourly example cou'd admi-
nifter. She foftered me, [*Weeps.*] and fhall I now
turn viper, and, with black ingratitude, fting the
tender heart that thus has cherifhed me? Shall I fe-
duce her houfe's heir, and kill her peace?—No; tho'
I lov'd to the mad extreme of female fondnefs—tho'
every worldly blifs, that woman's vanity, or man's
ambition cou'd defire, followed the indulgence of
my love; and all the contempt and mifery of this
life, the denial of that indulgence, I would difcharge
my duty to my benefactrefs, my earthly guardian, my
more than parent.

Egert. My dear Conftantia, your prudence, your
gratitude, and the cruel virtue of your felf-denial, do
but increafe my love, my admiration, and my mife-
ry.

Conft. Sir, I muft beg you will give me leave to return thefe bills and jewels.

Egert. Pray do not mention them—Sure my kindnefs and efteem may be indulged fo far, without fufpicion or reproach. I beg you will accept of them, nay, I infift.

Conft. I have done, fir—my ftation here is to obey—I know they are the gifts of a virtuous heart, and mine fhall convert them to the tendereft and moft grateful ufe—[*Weeps.*]

Egert. Hark! I hear a coach—it is my father—dear girl retire and compofe yourfelf—I will fend Sidney and my lady to you ; and by their judgment we will be directed. Will that fatisfy you?

Conft. I can have no will but my lady's—With your leave, I will retire—I would not fee her in this confufion.

Egert. Dear girl, adieu—and think of love, of happinefs, and the man, who never can be bleft without you.   [*Exit* Con.

Enter SAM.

Sam. Sir Pertinax, and my lady, are come, fir, and my lady defires to fpeak with you in her own room. O ! fhe is here, fir.   [*Exit* Sam.

Enter Lady MAC SYCOPHANT.

L. Mac. [*In great confufion and diftrefs.*] Dear child, I am glad to fee you, why did you not come to

town yefterday to attend the levee ? Your· father· is
incenfed to the uttermoft at your not being there.

Egert. [*In great warmth.*] Madam, it is with ex-
treme regret I tell you, that I can no longer be a flave
to his temper, his politics, and his fcheme of marrying
me to this woman.   Therefore, you had better con-
fent at once to my going out of the kingdom, and to
my taking Conftantia with me ; for without her, I
never can be l·appy.

L. Mac. As you regard my peace, or your own
charaêter, I beg you will not be guilty of fo rafh a
ftep.—You promifed me you would never· marry her
without my confent.   I will open it to your father—
Pray, dear Charles, be ruled, let me prevail.   Here
he comes, I will get out of his· way—but I beg,
Charles, while he is in this ill humour, that you will
not oppofe him, let him fay what he will—when his
paffion is a little cool, I will return and try to bring
him to reafon—but pray do not thwart him.

Egert. Madam, I will not.   [*Exit L. Mac.*

Enter Sir PERTINAX, *in great haughtinefs and anger.*

Sir Pert. Weel, fir, vary weel ! vary weel !—Are
not you a very fine fellow ; a hagh——

Enter TOMLINS.

What want you, fir ?

Tom. Sir, the groom is come back—he has been
as far as Hammerfmith, and the turnpike men, and

every perfon upon the road, are fure that Lord Lumbercourt has not paffed by this day.

Sir Pert. Let them take the chefnut gelding and return to town directly, and enquire at my lord's houfe, whether he is at home, or if they know what is become of him—and do you hear—the moment that Counfellor Plaufible and Mr. Serjeant Eitherfide arrive, let me know it. [*Exit Tomlins.*] Weel, fir, pray what do you think of yourfelf, are not you a fine fpark ?—are not you a fine fpark, I fay ?—So you would not come up to the levee ?

Egert. Sir, I beg your pardon, but I—I—I was not very well—befides, I did not think that my prefence there was neceffary.

Sir Pert. [*Snaps him up.*] Sir, it was neceffary—I tauld ye it was neceffary—and, fir, I muft now tell you, that the whole tenor of your conduct is moft offenfive.

Egert. I am forry you think fo, fir—I am fure I do not intend to offend you.

Sir Pert. I care not what you intend, fir, I tell you, you do offend—what is the meaning of this conduct ?—neglect the levee !—neglecting the levee is fuch a contempt, and fuch an ignorance of the world, that, 'fdeath, fir, your—What is your reafon, I fay, for thus neglecting the levee, and difobeying my commands ? [*Egerton bows.*] None of your bowing and fighing, fir, give me an immediate anfwer.

Egert. [*With a ftifled filial refentment.*] Sir, I own I am not ufed to levees ; nor do I know how to difpofe of myfelf, or what to fay or do in fuch a ftation.

Sir Per. With a proud angry reluctance—Zounds,
sir, do you not see, what others in genteel and impune;
temporal and spiritual: Lords, members, Judges,
Generals, and Bishops, aw crowding, worshipping, push-
ing foremost into the middle of the circle, and
there waiting, watching, and bowing at each a look
or a smile in the great Mon—which they meet with
an amicable familiarity of aspect, a modest cadence of
body, and a conciliating co-operation of the whole
mon, which expresses an officious promptitude for his
service, and indicates, that they look upon themselves
as the supplere appendage of his power, and the in-
listed Swiss of his political fortune.—This, sir, is
what you ought to do – and this, sir, is what I never
once omitted for these five and thirty years—let wha
wou'd be minister.

Egert. [*Afide.*] Contemptible!

Sir Pert. What is that ye mutter, sir?

Egert. Only a slight reflection, sir, not relative to
you.

Sir Pert. Sir, your absenting yourself from the
levee at this juncture, is suspeecious; it is luocked upon
as a kind of disaffection, and aw your country men are
highly offended with your conduct, for, sir, they do
not look upon you as a friend, or a well-wisher to.
Scotland, or to Scotchmen.

Egert. [*With a quick warmth.*] Then, sir, they
wrong me, I assure you; but pray, sir, in what par-
ticular can I be charged, either with coldness, or of-
fence to my country?

Sir Pert. Why, sir, ever since your mother's uncle
(Sir Stanly Egerton) left you this three thousand

pounds a year, and that you have, in compliance with his will, taken up the name of Egerton, they think you are growing proud, that you have eftranged your-felf fra the Mac Sycophants—have affociated with your mother's family—with the oppofeetion, and with thofe who do not wifh weel to Scotland—befides fir, in a converfation the other day after dinner, at your coufin Campbell M'Kenzie's before a whole table full of your ayn relations, did you not publicly wifh a total extinguifhment of aw party, and of aw national diftinctions whatever relative to the three kingdoms. [*With great anger.*] And was that a prudent wifh before fo many of your ain countrymen, and be damn'd to you ? Or was it a filial language to hold before me ?

Egert. Sir, with your pardon, I cannot think it un-filial or imprudent ; [*with a moft patriotic warmth.*] I own, I do wifh, moft ardently wifh, for a total ex-tinction of all parties ; particularly, that thofe of Eng-lifh, Irifh, and Scotch, might never more be brought into conteft or competition, unlefs like loving brothers, in general emulation for one common caufe.

Sir Pert. How, fir, do you perfift ? What would you banifh aw party and diftinction between Englifh, Irifh, and your ain countrymen ?

Egert. [*With great dignity of fpirit.*] I would, fir.

Sir Pert. Then damn ye, fir, ye are nai true Scot ! —Ay, fir, you may luock as angry as you wuol—but again, I fay—ye are nai true Scot !

Egert. Your pardon, fir, I think he is the true Scot, and the true citizen ; who wifhes equal juftice to the merit and demerit of every fubject of Great Britain, amongft whom, I know but of two diftinctions.

Sir Pert. Weel, fir,. and what are thofe? What are thofe ?

Egert. The knave, and the honeft man.

Sir Pert. Pfhaw ! ridiculous—nonfenfe !—ftuff !— all idle hacknied oppofition, cant, and nonfenfe.

Egert. And,. he, fir, who makes any other, be him of the North, or of the South, of the Eaft, or of the Weft, in place,. or out of place ; is an enemy to the whole, and to the virtues of humanity !

Sir Pert. Ay, fir, this is your brother's impudent doctrine—for the which I have banifhed him for ever fra. my prefence, my heart, and my fortune. — Sir, I will have nai fon of mine, becaufe truly he has been educated in an Englifh feminary. prefume (under the mafk of public candor) to fpeak againft his native land, or my principles, fir—Scotfmen —Scotfmen—fir, wherever they meet throughout the globe fhould unite and ftick together, as it were in a political phalanx.

Egert. That is a fevere judgment, fir, and according to my obfervation, and indeed my frequent experience, confiftent neither with truth, nor the indifcriminate affection of impartial nature.

Sir Pert. How, fir, not confiftent with truth ?

Egert. Not in my opinion, fir, for I, who am a Scotchman as well as you, have met with as warm friendfhips, and as many too, out of Scotland, as ever I met with in it.

Sir Pert. Sir, I do not believe you !—I do not believe you !—But, fir, you have a faucy, lurking prejudice againft your ain country, you hate it—yes, your mother, her family, and your brother, fir, have aw

the fame difaffected rankling, and by that, and their
politics together, they will be the ruin of you, them-
felves, and aw' who connect with them: however,
nai mair of that now, I weel talk at large with ye
about that bufinefs anon.—In the mean time, fir, not-
withftanding your contempt of my advice, and your
difobedience till my commands, I will convince you
of my paternal attention till your welfare, by my ma-
nagement with this voluptuary—this Lord Lumber-
court, whofe daughter you are to marry—ye ken, fir,
that the fellow has been my patron thefe three and
thirty years.

Egert. True, fir.

Sir Pert. Vary weel—and now, fir, you fee by his
prodigality, he is become my dependant, and accord-
ingly, I have made my bargain with him. The dee'l a
baubee he has in the world, but what comes thro'
thefe clutches; for his whole eftate, which has three
impleecit boroughs on it, mark—is now in my cuftody
at nurfe; the which eftate, on my paying off his debts,
and allowing him a life-rent of feven thoufand pounds
per annum, is to be made over till me for my life; and
at my death it is to defcend till ye, and your iffue.—
The peerage of Lumbercourt, ye ken, will follow of
courfe.—So, fir, ye fee by this marriage there are
three impleecit boroughs, the whole patrimoney of
Lumbercourt, and a peerage at one flap—Why it is a
ftroke—a hit—a hit.—Zounds, fir, a man may live a
century and not make fic another hit again.

Egert. It is a very advantageous bargain, no doubt,
fir—But what will my Lord's family fay to it?

Sir Pert. Why, man, he cares not, if his family
were aw at the dee'l, fo that his luxury be but grati-
fied.—Only let him have a race horfe till feed his va-
nity, his polite blacklegs to advife him in his matches
on the turf, at cards, and at tenis, and his harridan
till drink drams woe him, and in her drunken hyfterics
to fcrat his face and burn his periwig, or let him have
a dozen of his dependants, and half a dozen of his
Swifs borough voters, fit up all night drinking bumpers
of fuccefs to the oppofition—and double bumpers of
deftruction to the miniftry; and then, fir, the fellow
has aw that he wants, and aw that he wifhes in this
world or the next.

Enter TOMLINS.

Tom. Lady Rodolpha is come, fir.

Sir Pert. And my lord?

Tom. Sir, he is about a mile or two behind, the
fervants fay.

Sir Pert. Let me know the inftant he arrives.

Tom. I fhall, fir.   [*Exit.*

Sir Pert. Step ye oot, Charles, and receive lady
Rodolpha—and I defire, fir, that you wool treat her
with as much refpact and gallantry afs poffible; for
my lord has hinted that ye have been a little remifs
afs a lover—So go, go, and receive her with warmth
and rapture.

Egert. I fhall, fir.

Sir Pert. Odzucks, Charles, you fhou'd adminif-
ter a torrent of adulation to her; for women, fir,
never thinks a man loves her till he has made an idiot
of her underftanding by flattery—for flattery, fir, is

the prime blifs of the fex—the nectar and ambrofia
of their vanity, fo that you can never give them too
much of it—go, go, a good lad, and mind your
flattery. [*Exit Egerton.*] Ha ! I muft keep a tight
hand upon this fellow, I fee—ah ! I am frightened
out of my wits left his mother's family fhould feduce
him to the oppofition party, which would totally ruin
my whole fcheme, and break my heart—a fine time
a day, indeed, for a blockhead till turn patriot—
when the character is exploded—marked—pro-
fcribed ; why the common people, the very vulgar
have found out the jeft, and laugh at a patriot now
a days juft as they do at a magician, a conjuror, or any
other impoftor in fociety. .

Enter Tomlins *and Lord* Lumbercourt.

Tom. Lord Lumbercourt.   [*Exit* Tom.

L. Lum. Sir Pertinax, I kifs your hand.

Sir Pert. [*Bows very low.*] Your lordfhip's moft
devoted—l rejoice to fee you.

L. Lum. Why you ftole a march on me this morn-
ing—gave me the flip, Mac, tho' I never wanted your
affiftance more in my life, I thought you would have
called upon me

Sir Pert. My dear lord I beg ten millions of par-
dons for leaving the town before you ; but you ken
that your lordfhip at dinner yefterday pofitively fet-
tled it, that we fhould meet this morning at the
levee.

L. Lum. That I acknowledge, Mac—I did promife to be there, I own.

Sir Pert. You did, indeed, and accordingly I was at the levee, and waiting there till every mortal was gone—and feeing you did not come, I concluded that your lordfhip was gone before, and away I pelted hither, as I thought after ye.

L. Lum. Why, to confefs the truth, my dear Mac—that old finner, Lord Freakifh, General Jolly, Sir Anthony Soker, and two or three more of that fet, laid hold of me laft night at the opera; and as the general fays, I believe by the intelligence of my head this morning, that we drank deep ere we departed—ha! ha! ha!

Sir Pert. Ha! ha! ha! Nay, if you were with that party, my lord, I don't wonder at not feeing your lordfhip at the levee.

L. Lum. The truth is, Sir Pertinax, my fellow let me fleep too long for the levee; but I wifh I had feen you before you left town, I wanted you dreadfully.

Sir Pert. I am heartily forry then I was not in the way, but on what account my lord did you want me?

L. Lum. Ha! ha! ha! a curfed awkard affair—and ha! ha! ha! yet, I cannot help laughing at it neither—tho' it vexed me confoundedly.

Sir Pert. Vexed you my lord! Zounds, I wifh I had been with you—but for heaven's fake, my lord, what was it that could poffibly vex your lordfhip?

L. Lum. Why that impudent, teazing, dunning

rafcal, Mahogany, my upholfterer---you know the fellow.

Sir Pert. Perfectly, my lord.

L. Lum. This impudent fcoundrel has fued me up to fome kind of a fomething or other in the law, which I think they call---an execution.

Sir Pert. The rafcal.

L. Lum. Upon which, fir, the fellow, by way of afking pardon, had the modefty of waiting upon me two or three days ago, to inform my *honour*, ha! ha! ha! as he was pleafed to dignify me, that the execution was now ready to put in force againft my *honour*, but that out of refpect to my *honour*, as he had taken a great deal of my *honour's* money, he would not fuffer his lawyer to ferve it upon my *honour*, till he had firft informed my *honour*, becaufe he was not willing to affront my *honour*--ha! ha! ha!---a fon of a whore.

Sir Pert. I never heard of fo impudent a dog!

L. Lum. Now my dear Mac---ha! ha!. ha! as the fcoundrel's apology was fo very fatisfactory---and his information fo very agreeable, I told him that in *honour*, I thought that my *honour*, could not do lefs than to order his *honour* to be paid immediately.

Sir Pert. Vary weel---vary weel---ye were as complaifant as the fcoundrel till the full, I think, my lord.

L. Lum. You fhall hear---you fhall hear, Mac---So, fir, with great compofure, feeing a fmart oaken cudgel, that ftood very handily in a corner of my dreffing room, I ordered two of my fellows to hold the raf-

C

cal, and another to take the cudgel, and return the scoundrel's civility with a good drubbing, as long as the stick lasted.

Sir Pert. Ha! ha! ha! admirable—afs gude a stroke of humour and fun as ever I heard of—And did they drub him, my lord?

L. Lum. O! moft liberally—ha! ha! ha!—moft liberally, fir—and there I thought the affair would have refted, till I fhou'd think proper to pay the fcoundrel; but this morning, fir, juft as I was ftepping into my chaife—my fervants all about me, a fellow, called a tip-ftaff, ftept up to us, and with a very modeft addrefs, requefted the favour of my *footman*, who thrafhed the upholfterer, and the two that held him, to go along with him, upon a little bufinefs—to my Lord Chief Juftice.

Sir Pert. The Devil!

L. Lum. And at the very fame inftant, I in my turn, was accofted by two very civil fcoundrels, who, with a moft infolent politenefs, begged my pardon, and informed me, that I muft not go into my own chaife.

Sir Pert. How, my lord, not into your ain carriage?

L. Lum. No, fir, not into my own chaife, for that they, by order of the fheriff, muft feize it at the fuit of a gentleman, one Mr. Mahogony, an upholfterer.

Sir Pert. An impudent villain!

L. Lum. It is all true, I affure you, fo you fee my dear Mac, what a damn'd country this is to live in! where noblemen are obliged to pay their debts, juft like merchants, coblers, peafants, or mechanics—is not that a damn'd fcandal to the nation, Mac?

Sir Pert. Sir, there is not a nation in the whole world befides, has fuch a grievance to complain of.

L. Lum. But, fir, what is worfe than all that, the fcoundrel has feized upon the houfe too, that I furnifhed for the girl I took from the opera.

Sir Pert. I never heard of fic an a fcoundrel!

L. Lum. Ay, but what concerns me moft, my dear Mac, is, I am afraid that the villain will fend down to New-market, and feize my ftring of horfes.

Sir Pert. Your ftring of horfes! Zounds! we muft prevent that at all events—that would be fuch a difgrace—I will difpatch an exprefs to town directly, to put a ftop till the fcoundrel's proceedings.

L. Lum. Prithee do, my dear Sir Pertinax.

Sir Pert. O! it fhall be done, my Lord.

L. Lum. Thou art an honeft fellow, upon honour.

Sir Pert. O! my lord, it is my duty to oblige your lordfhip, to the utmoft ftretch of my abeelity.

Enter TOMLINS.

Tom. Colonel Toper, prefents his compliments to you, fir, and having no family down with him in the country, he, and Captain Hardbottle, if not inconvenient, wil do themfelves the *honour* of taking a family dinner with you.

Sir Pert. They are two of our militia officers— does your lordfhip know them?

L. Lum. By fight only.

Sir Pert. I am afraid, my lord, they will interrupt our bufinefs.

L. Lum. Not at all—I fhould like to be acquainted with Toper ; they fay he's a damn'd jolly fellow.

Sir Pert. O, devilifh jolly !—devilifh jolly !—he and the captain are twa of the hardeft drinkers in the country.

L. Lum. So I have heard ; let us have them by all means, Mac—they will enliven the fcene. How far are they from you ?

Sir Pert. Juft acrofs the meadows—not half a mile my lord ; a ftep, a ftep.

L. Lum. O, let us have the jolly dogs, by all means.

Sir Pert. My compliments—I fhall be proud of their company. [*Exit Tomlins.*] Guif you pleafe, my lord, we will gang, and chat a bit with the women ; I have not feen Lady Rodolpha fince fhe returned fra Bath, I long to have a leetle news fra her aboot the company there.

L. Lum. O ! fhe'll give you an account of them, I warrant you. [*Loud laugh within.*]

Lady Rodolpha, [*Within.*] Ha ! ha ! ha !—Well, I vow, coufin Egerton, you have a vaft deal of fhrewd humour.

L. Lum. Here the hair brain comes—it muft be her by the noife.

Lady Rodol. [*Within.*] Allons, gude folks—follow me—fans ceremonie !——

Enter Lady RODOLPHA, *Lady* MAC SYCOPHANT,
EGERTON, *and* SIDNEY.

L Rodol. [*Running up to Sir Pert.*] Sir Pertinax---
your moſt devoted---moſt obſequious, and moſt obedi-
ent vaſſal. [*Curtſeys very low.*]

Sir Pert. Lady Rodolpha---doon till the graund,
my congratulations, duty, and affection, are at your
devotion ; and I ſhould rejoice till kiſs your ladyſhip's
footſteps. [*Bows ridiculouſly low.*]

L. Rodol. O, Sir Pertinax, your humility is moſt
ſublimely complaiſant---at preeſent---unanſwerable ;---
but, ſir, I ſhall inſtantly ſtudy to return it faſty fold.
[*Curtſeys very low*]

Sir Pert. Your ladyſhip does me a ſingular honour
---weel, madam---ha ! you luock gaily---weel, and
how, how is your ladyſhip, after your jaunt till the
Bath ?

L. Rodol. Never better, Sir Pertinax ! as weel as
youth, health, riotous ſpirits, and a careleſs, happy
heart can make me.

Sr Pert. I am mighty glad till hear it, my lady.

L. Lum. Ay, ay, Rodolpha is always in ſpirits, Sir
Pertinax---vive la bagatelle---is the happy philoſophy
of our family---ha ! Rodolpha---ha !

L. Rodol. Traith is it my lord ; and upon honour,
I am determined it never ſhall be changed by my con-
ſent, ha ! ha ! ha !---weel, I vow, vive la bagatelle,
would be a moſt brilliant motto for the chariot of a

belle of fashion---what say you till my fancy, Lady
Mac Sycophant ?·

L. Mac. It wou'd have novelty at least to recom-
mend it, madam.

L. Rodol. Which of ay chairms! is the most de-
lightful ! that can accompany wit, taste, love, or
friendship : for novelty I take to be the true *je-ne-
sçais-quoi* of all worldly blifs. Coufin Egerton, should
not you wish to have a wife, with vive la bagatelle,
upon her chariot.

Egert. O, certainly, madam.

L. Rodol. Yes, I think it wou'd be new, quite out
of the common, and singularly elegant.

Egert. Indisputably so, madam---for as a motto is a
word to the wife, or rather a broad hint to the whole
world, of a perfon's taste and principles---vive la baga-
telle ! would be most expreffive, at first fight, of your
ladyship's mental character.

L. Rodol. O ! master Egerton ! you touch my very
heart we your approbation !---ha ! ha ! ha ! yes---vive
la bagatelle, is the very spirit of my intention, the in-
stant I commence bride ! Well, I'm immensely·proud
that my fancy has the approbation of so found an un-
derstanding, and so polished a taste---afs *that* of the
all-accomplished Mr. Egerton.   [*Curtseys very
low.*]

Egert. O ! Heavens, madam, your ladyship's pa-
negyric is most superlatively complaffant---to anfwer
it, madam, would require the afcendancy of the high-
est heaven of invention, and of its brightest sublimi-
ty.

ACT II.   MAN OF THE WORLD.   39

L. Rodol. Weel, I vow mafter Egerton, you have a moft aftonifhing genius in the complimentary ftyle; not to be decyphered by the prefent ftate of my inexperienced capacity!—but, fir, in order to improve and elevate my intellects, I am determined in a few months to commence a long voyage of air balloon philofophy, on purpofe to learn the complimentary fublime, in imitation of mafter Egerton, that great luminary of wit, humour, and all convivial politenefs!

L. Lum. Hey day, hey day! what the devil are ye both about, with your higheft heavens, your air balloons, your fublimity, and your nonfenfical jargon: You feem to me, to be playing at riddle my riddle my ree—tell me what my nonfenfe fhall be; it is all downright jargon, upon honour, I do not underftand a fingle thought of all you have both uttered.

Sir Pert But I do—I do—and they'll foon underftand yan another—But, Lady Rodolpha, I wanted till afk your ladyfhip fome queftions aboot the company at Bath---they fay ye had aw the world there.

L. Rodol. O yes, there was a very great mob, indeed —but vary little company:—aw canaille—except our ain party—the place was quite crooded with your little purfe proud mechanics, an odd kind of queer luocking animals, that hai ftarted intul fortune, fra lottery tickets, rich prizes at fea, gambling at Change-alley, and fic caprices of fortune—and awa they aw crood till the Bath.

Sir Pert. Ha! ha! admirable! what a fund of entertainment!

L. Rodol. O, fuperlative, and inexhauftible, Sir Per-
tinax, ha! ha! ha!—Madam, we haud in yane
group, a peer, and a fharper—a duchefs, and a pin-
maker's wife—a boarding fchool mifs, and her grand-
mother—a fat parfon, a lean general, and a yellow
admiral—ha! ha! ha! aw fpeaking together, and
bawling, and wrangling, and jangling, and fretting,
and fuming, in fierce contention, afs if the fame and
fortune of aw the partiés were to be iffue of the con-
flict.

Sir Pert. Ha! ha! ha! excellent, and pray,
madam, what was the object of their fierce contenti-
on?

L. Rodol. O! a vary important one I affure you!—
of no lefs confequence, madam, than how an odd trick
at whift was loft—or might have been faved—ha!
ha! ha!

Omnes. Ha! ha! ha!

L. Mac. Ridiculous.

L. Lum. Ha! ha! ha! My dear Rodolpha, I have
feen that very conflict a thoufand times.

Sir Pert. And fo have I, upon my honour, my
lord.

L. Rodol. In another party, Sir Pertinax, ha! ha!
ha! we had what was called the cabinet council!
which was compofed of a duke, and a haberdafher; a
red hot patriot, and a fneering courtier; a difcarded
ftatefman, and his fcribbling chaplain;—we a bufy,
brawling, muckle-heeded prerogative lawyer—aw of
whom were every minute ready to gang together by
the lugs, aboot the in and the oot meeniftry. Ha!
ha! ha!

Sir Pert. Ha! ha! ha!—Weel, that is a droll motley cabinet, I vow, vary whimfical upon my honour—but they are aw great poleeticions at Bath, and fettle a meeniftry there with afs much eafe afs they do a tune for a country dance!

L. Rodol. Then, Sir Pertinax, in a retired part of the room, fnug in a bye corner, in clofe conference, we haud a Jew and a beefhop.

Sir Pert. A Jew and beefhop—ha! ha! a devilifh good connexion, that—and pray, my lady, what were they aboot?

L. Rodol. Why, fir, the beefhop was ftriving to convert the Jew—while the Jew, by intervals, was flyly picking up intelligence fra the beefhop aboot the change in the meeniftry, in hopes of making a ftroke in the ftocks.

Omnes. Ha! ha! ha!

Sir Pert. Admirable! admirable! I honour the fmoufe—ha! ha! ha! it was deevilifh clever—the Jew diftilling the beefhop's brains.

L. Lum. Yes, yes, the fellow kept a fharp look out; it was a fair trial of fkill on both fides, Mr. Egerton.

Egert. True, my lord, but the Jew feems to be in the faireft way to fucceed.

L. Lum. O all to nothing, fir, ha! ha! ha!— Well, child, I like your Jew and your bifhop much. It is devilifh clever, let us have the reft of the hiftory, pray my dear.

L. Rodol. Gude traith, my lord, the fum total is, that there we aw daunced, and wrangled, and flattered, and flandered, and gambled, and cheated, and mingled, and jumbled, and walloped together, till my very bowels went crack again with the woolley wambles.

Omnes. Ha! ha! ha!

L. Lum. Ha! ha! ha!—Well, you are a droll girl, Rodolpha, and upon honour-- ha! ha! ha! you have given us as whimfical a fketch as ever was hit off.

Sir Pert. A yes, my lord, it is an excellent peecture of the oddities that one meets with at Bath.

L. Lum. Why yes, I think there is fome fancy in it, Egerton.

Egert. Very characteriftic, indeed, my lord.

L. Lum. What fay you, Mr. Sidney? Don't you think there is fomething fprightly in her dafhing Caledonian genius?

Sid. Upon my word, my lord, the lady has made me fee the whole affembly in diftinct colours.

L. Lum. Ho! ho! ho! you indelicate creature— why, my dear Rodolpha, ha! ha! ha! do you know what you are talking about?

L. Rodol. Weel, weel, my lord, guin you lough rill you burft, the fact is ftill true; now in Ederburgh, my lady, in Edenburgh we ha nai fic pinchgut doings, for there gude traith, we always hai a gude oomfortable difh of cutlets, or collops, or a nice warm, favorey haggis, we a gude fwag o' whafkey punch till recruit our fpeerits, aufter our dauncing and fwatting.

Omnes. Ha! ha! ha!

Sir Pert. Ay, that is much wholfomer, Lady Rodolpha, than aw their flips and flaps here, i' th' footh.

L. Lum. Ha! ha! ha!---Well, my dear Rodolpha, you are a droll girl; upon honour, and very entertaining, I vow---but, my dear child, a little too much upon the dancing and fweating, and the woolley wambles.

Omnes. Ha ! ha ! ha !

Enter TOMLINS.

Tom Colonel Toper, and Captain Hardbottle, are come, fir.

Sir Pert. O, vary weel, dinner immediately.

Tom. It is ready, fir.   [*Exit* Tom.

Sir Pert. My lord, we attend your lordfhip.

L. Lum. Lady Mac---your ladyfhip's hand, if you pleafe. [*Leads her out.*]

Sir Pert. Lady Rodolpha, here is a fighing arcadian fwain, that, I believe, has a hand at your ladyfhip's devotion.

L. Rodol. And I, Sir Pertinax, hai yean at his.--- There, fir, [*Gives her hand to Egerton*] as to hearts ye ken coufin, they are no brought into the account of human dealings now a days.

Egert O, madam, they are meer temporary baubles, efpecially in courtfhip, and no more to be depended on, than the weather, or a lottery ticket.

L. Rodol. Ha ! ha ! ha ! twa excellent fimilies I vow, Mr. Egerton---excellent, for they illuftrate the

vagaries and inconftancy of my diffipated heart, afs
exactly afs if ye had meant till defcribe it. [*Egerton
leads her off.*]

Sir Pert. Ha! ha! h'a! what a vaft fund of fpee-
rits and guid-humour fhe has, Maifter Sidney.

Sid. A great fund, indeed, Sir Pertinax.

Sir Pert. Come let us till dinner---ha! by this time
to-morrow, Maifter Sidney, I hope we fhall have every
thing ready for ye to put the laft hand to the hap-
pinefs of your friend and pupil---and then, fir, my
cares will be over for this life---for as till my other fon
Sandy, I expect nai gude of him, nor fhould I grieve
were I to fee him in his coffin. But this match—O!
it will make me the happieft of aw human beings!

[*Exeunt.*

ACT III. SCENE I.

Enter Sir PERTINAX and EGERTON.

Sir Pertinax.

ZOONDS, fir, I will not hear a word aboot it.---I in-
fift upon it ye were wrong---ye fhai'd hai paid your
court till my lord, and not hai fcrupled fwallowing a
bumper, or twa, or twanty, till oblige him.

Egert. Sir, I did drink his toaſt in a bumper.

Sir Pert. Yas, ye did; but how? how? Juſt aſs a bairn takes pheeſye, we averſion, and wry faces, whach my lord obſerved.   Then to mend the maiter, the moment that he and the colonel get intill a drunken diſpute aboot religion, ye ſlily ſlunged awa.

Egert. I thought, ſir, it was time to go, when my lord inſiſted upon half-pint bumpers.

Sir Pert. That was not levell'd at you, but at the colonel, in order till try his bottom---but they all agreed that ye and I ſhou'd drink out of ſmall glaſſes.

Egert. But, ſir, I beg pardon---I did not chuſe to drink any more.

Sir Pert. But zoonds, ſir! I tell you there was a neceſſity for your drinking more.

Egert. A neceſſity! in what reſpeſt, ſir?

Sir Pert. Why, ſir, I have a certain point to carry, independent of the lawyers, with my lord, in this agreement of your marriage, aboot which I am afraid we ſhall hai a warm ſquabble, and therefore I wanted your aſſiſtance in it.

Egert. But how, ſir, could my drinking contribute to aſſiſt you in your ſquabble?

Sir Pert. Yas, ſir, it would hai contributed, and greatly hai contributed till aſſiſt me.

Egert. How ſo, ſir?

Sir Pert. Nai, ſir, it might hai prevented the ſquabble entirely, for as my lord is prood of ye for a ſon-in-law, and of your little French ſongs, your ſtories, about the popes, and cardinals, and their miſtreſſes, and your bon mots, when ye are in the humour, and

guin you had but ftaid and been a leetle jolly, and
drank half a fcore bumpers we him, till he got a little
tipfy, I am fure when we had him i' that mood, we
might ha fettled the point among ourfelves before the
lawyers come ; but noo, fir, I donna ken what will be
the confequence.

Egert. But, when a man is intoxicated, would that
have been a feafonable time to fettle bufinefs, fir ?

Sir Pert. The moft feafonable—-the moft feafonable
—-for, fir, when my lord is in his cups, his fufpeecion
is afleep, and his heart is aw jolity, feen, and gude
fellowfhip-—and, fir, can there be a happier moment
than that for a bargain, or till fettle a difpute we a
friend ? What is that you fhrug your fhoulders at, fir ?
—-and turn up your eyes to heaven, like a duck in
thunder !

Egert. At my own ignorance, fir—for I underftand
neither the philofophy, nor the morality of your doc-
trine.

Sir Pert. I know you do not, fir—and what is
worfe, ye never weel underftand it, as long afs ye
proceed.—In yean word, Chairles, I hai often tauld
ye, and again I tell ye, yeance for aw, that the ma-
nœuvres of pleeabeelity are as neceffary to rife i' the
world, afs wrangling and logical fubtilty at the bar—
why, you fee, fir, I hai acquired a noble fortune—
a princely fortune—and how d'ye think I raifed
it ?

Egert. Doubtlefs, fir, by your abilities.

Sir Pert. Dootlefs, fir, ye are a blockhead—Nae,
Sir, I'll tell you how I raifed it, fir—I raifed it by,

boowing—by boowing, fir.—I never i' my life could
ftand ftraight i' the prefence of a great man ; but was
aw ways booing, and booing, and booing—afs—afs—
if it were by inftinct.

Egert. How do you mean by inftinct, fir ?

Sir Pert. How do I mean by inftinct ; why, fir, I
mean by—by—by the inftinct of intereft, fir, which
is the univerfal inftinct of mankind, fir ; it is wonder-
ful to think what a cordial, what an amicable, nay,
what an infaleeble influence, booing has upon the pride
and vanity of human nature—Chairles, anfwer me
fincerely, hai ye a mind till be convinced of the force
of my doctrine, by example and demonftration ?

Egert. Certainly, fir.

Sir Pert. Then, fir, as the greateft favour I can con-
fer upon you, I will gi ye a fhort fketch of the ftages of
my boowing, afs an excitement, and a land-mark for
ye till boow by, and afs an infaleeble noftrum for a
man of the world, till thrive in the world.

Egert. Sir, I fhall be proud to profit by your expe-
rience.

Sir Pert. Vary weel, fir—fit ye down then, [*Both
fit.*] and now, fir, you muft recall till your thoughts,
that your grandfather was a man whofe penurious in-
come of captain's half-pay, was the fum total of his for-
tune ; and, fir, aw my proveefion fra him, was a mo-
dicum of Latin, an expartnefs at areethmatic, and a
fhort fyftem of worldly counfel, the chief ingredients
of whach were, a perfevering induftry—a reegid œco-
nomy—a fmooth tongue—a pliabeelity of temper—
and a conftant attention till make every great man
well pleafed we himfelf.   ⁚⁚

Egert. Very prudent conduct, sir.

Sir Pert. Therefore, sir, I lay it before ye.—Now, sir, wi thefe materials, I fet out a rough, rawboned ftrippling fra the north, till try my fortune we them here i' the footh—and my firft ftep intull the world, was a beggarly clerkfhip in Sawney Gordon's coonting-houfe, here in the city of London, whach you'll fay afforded but a barren fort of a profpect.

Egert. It was not a very fertile one, indeed, sir.

Sir Pert. The reverfe—the reverfe—weel, sir, feeing my fel in this unprofitable feetuation, I reflacted deeply. I caft aboot my thoughts, and concluded that a matrimonial adventure, prudently conducted, would be the readieft gate I could gang for the bettering of my condition, and accordingly I fet aboot it ; now, sir, in this purfuit—beauty—beauty—ah ! beauty often ftruck mine een, and played aboot my heart —and fluttered, and beat, and knocked—and knocked—but the deel an entrance I ever let it get—for I obferved, that beauty is generally a prood, vain, faucy, expenfive fort of a commodity.

Egert. Very juftly obferved, sir.

Sir Pert. And therefore I left it to the prodigals and coxcombs, that could afford till pay for it, and its ftead, sir, mark—I luock'd oot for an antient, well jointered, fuperanuated dowager—a confumptive, toothlefs, ptifical, wealthy widow—or a fhreeveled, cadaverous, neglected piece of deformity, i' the fhape of an eezard, or an apperfiand—or in fhort, any thing —any thing that had the filler—the filler—for that was the north ftar of my affection ; do you take me, sir—was nai that right ?

Egert. O doubtlefs, doubtlefs, fir.

Sir Pert. Now, fir, where do ye think I ganged to luock for this woman we the filler ? Nai till court—nai till play-houfes, nor affemblies—nai, fir, I ganged till the kirk—till the anabaptift, eendependant, bradleonian, muckletonian meetings—till the morning and evening fervice of churches and chapples of eafe—and till the midnight, melting, conciliating love-feafts of the methodifts—and there, at laft, fir, I fell upon an old, rich, fower, flighted, antiquated, mufty maiden. She was as tall as a grenadier, and fo thin that fhe luocked, ha! ha! ha! fhe luocked—juft like a fkeleton in a furgeon's glafs cafe—Now, fir, this meeferable object, was releegioufly angry wi herfelf, and aw the world—and had nai comfort but in a fupernatural, vicious, and enthufiaftic delirums; ha! ha! ha! fir, fhe was mad—afs mad as a bedla-mite.

Egert. Not impoffible, fir—there are numbers of peor creatures in the fame condition.

Sir Pert O numbers, numbers—now, fir, this cracked creature ufed to pray, and fing, and figh, and groan, and weep, and wail, and gnafh her teeth conftantly, morning and evening, at the tabernacle in Moor-fields, and as foon as I found fhe had the filler, aha !—in gude truth, I plumpt me doon upon my knees, clofe by her, cheek by jole, and praid, and fighed, and groaned, and gnafhed my teeth, as vehemently afs fhe could do for the life of her—ay, and turned up the whites of mine een, till the ftrings awmoft crackt again—Weel, fir, I watched her motions—

handed her till her chair—waited on her home—got moft releegioufly intimate we her—in a week married her—in a fortnight buried her—in a month touched the filler—and we a deep fuit of mourning, a melancholy port, a forrowful veefage, and a joyful heart, I began the world again—and this, fir, was the firft effectual boow I ever made, till the vanity of human nature.——Now, fir, d'ye underftand this doctrine ?

Egert. Perfectly well, fir.

Sir Pert. Ay, boot was it not right ? Was it not ingenious, and weel hit off ?

Egert. Extremely well, fir.

Sir Pert. My next boow, fir, was till your ain meether, whom I ran away wi fra the boarding fchool —by the intereft of whofe family, I got a good fmart place in the treafury—and, fir, my vary next ftep was intill Parliament—the whach I entered we as ardent, and afs determined an ambeetion afs ever agitated the heart o' Ceafer himfelf!—and then, fir, I changed my character entirely.—Sir, I boowed, and watched, and harkened, and lurked for intilligence, and ran aboot backwards and forwards, and attended, and dangled upon the then great mon, till I got intill the very boowels of his confeedence; and then, fir, I wriggled, and wriggled, and wrought, and wriggled till I wriggled myfelf among the vary thick o' them, till I got my fnack of the cloathing, the foraging, the contracts, the lottery teeckets, and aw the poleetical bonuffes—till at length, fir, I became a much wealthier mon, than one-half o' the golden calves I had been fo

long a boowing to. [*He rifes, Egerton rifes too.*]
And was not that boowing to fome purpofe, fir?—
Ha!

Egert. It was indeed, fir.

Sir Pert. But are you convinced of the gude effeꝼts,
and of the uteelity of boowing?

Egert. Thoroughly, fir, thoroughly.

Sir Pert. Sir, it is infaleeble—but, Chairles, ah!
While I was thus boowing, and wriggling, and making
a princely fortune—ah! I met many heart fores, and
difappointments frai the want of leeterature, ailo-
quence, and other popular abeelities. Sir, guin I could
hai both fpoken i' the houfe, I fhou'd hai done the
deed in half the time—boot the inftant I opened my
mouth there, they aw fell a laughing at me—aw
whach deefeeciencies, fir, I determined at any expence
till hai fupplied by the polifhed education of a fon,
who, I hoped, wou'd yean day raife the houfe of
Mac Sycophant till the higheft pannicle of meeneefte-
rial ambeetion.—This, fir, is my plan, I hai done my
part of it, nature has done hers—Ye are ailoquent, ye
are popular—aw parties like ye—and noow, fir, it
only remains for ye to be direꝼted—completion fol-
lows.

Egert. Your liberality, fir, in my education, and the
judicious choice you made of the worthy gentleman,
to whofe virtues and abilities you entrufted me, are
obligations I fhall ever remember, with the deepeft filial
gratitude.

Sir Pert. Vary weel, fir—vary weel—but, Chairles,
hai ye haid any converfation yet we Lady Rodolpha,

aboot the day of your marriage, your laveries, your equeepage, or your eftablifhment ?

Egert. Not yet, fir.

Sir Pert. Pah! why, there again noow—ye are wrong, vary wrong.

Egert. Sir, we have not had an opportunity.

Sir Pert. Why, Chairles, ye are very tardy in this bufinefs.

> [*Lord Lumbercourt fings without, flufbed with wine.*
> *What have we with day to do,*
> *Sons of Care 'twas made for you.*]

Sir Pert. O! here comes my lord.

L. Lumb. [*Sings without.*] Sons of Care 'twas made for you.

Enter Lord LUMBERCOURT, *drinking a cup of coffee,* TOMLINS *waiting with a falver.*

L. Lum. Sons of care 'twas made for you —Very good coffee indeed, Mr. Tomlins. Here, Mr. Tomlins. [*Gives the cup.*]

Tom. Will your lordfhip pleafe to have another difh ?

L. Lum. No, thank ye, Mr. Tomlins. [*Exit Tomlins.*] Well, my hoft of Scotch pints, we have had warm work.

Sir Pert. Yes, you pufhed the bottle aboot my lord wi the joy and veegar of a bacchanal.

L. Lum. That I did, my dear Mac—no lofs o time with me—I have but three motions old boy—

charge—toaft—fire, and off we go—ha! ha! ha!
that's my exercife.

Sir Pert. And fine warm exercife it is, my lord, ef-
pecially with the half pint bumpers.

L. Lum. Zounds! it does execution point blank.
Ay, ay, none of your pimping acorn glaffes for me, but
your manly, old Englifh half pint bumpers my dear.
Zounds! fir, they try a fellow's ftamina at once—
But where's Egerton?

Sir Pert. Juft at hand, my lord—there he ftands,
luocking at your lordfhip's picture.

L. Lum. My dear Egerton!——

Egert. Your lordfhip's moft obedient.

L. Lum. I beg pardon, I did not fee you—I am
forry you left us fo foon after dinner—had you ftaid,
you would have been highly entertained, I have made
fuch examples of the commiffioner, the captain, and
the colonel.

Egert. So I underftand, my lord.

L. Lum. But, Egerton, I have flipt from company
for a few moments on purpofe to have a little chat
with you.   Rodolpha tells me, fhe fancies there is a
kind of demur on your fide, about your marriage with
her.

Sir Pert. A demur; how fo, my lord?

L. Lum. Why, as I was drinking my coffee with
the women juft now, I defired they wou'd fix the
wedding night, and the etiquette of the ceremony,
upon which the girl burft into a loud laugh, telling
me fhe fuppofed I was joking, for that Mr. Egerton

had never yet given a fingle glance or hint upon the fubject.

Sir Pert. My lord, I have juft now been talking till him aboot his fhynefs till the lady.

Enter TOMLINS.

Tom. Counfellor Plaufible is come, fir, and Serjeant Eitherfide.

Sir Pert. Why then we can fettle the bufinefs this very evening, my lord.

L. Lum. As well as in feven years—and to make the way as fhort as poffible, pray Mafter Tomlins, prefent your mafter's compliments and mine to Lady Rodolpha, and let her ladyfhip know we wifh to fpeak with her directly. [*Exit* Tom.] He fhall attack her this inftant, Sir Pertinax.

Sir Pert. Ay, this is doing bufinefs effectually, my lord.

L. Lum. O! we will pit them in a moment, Sir Pertinax. That will bring them into the heat of the action at once, and fave a deal of awkardnefs on both fides.—O! here your Dulcinea comes.

Enter Lady RODOLPHA *finging, a mufic book in her hand.*

L. Rodol. I have been learning this air of Conftantia; I proteft her touch on the harpfichord is quite brilliant, and really her voice not amifs. Weel, Sir,

Pertinax, I attend your commands, and your's my paternal lord. [*She curtseys very low, and my lord bows very low, and answers her in the same tone and manner.*

L. Lum. Why then, my filial lady, we are to inform you, that the commission for your ladyship, and this enamoured cavalier, commanding you jointly and separately to serve your country in the honourable and forlorn hope of matrimony, is to be signed this very evening.

L. Rodol. This evening, my lord !

L. Lum. This evening, my lady—Come, Sir Pertinax, let us leave them to settle their liveries, wedding suits, carriages, and all their amorous equipage for the nuptial camp.

Sir Pert. Ha! ha! ha! excellent, excellent—well I vow, my lord, ye are a great officer, this is as gude a manœuver to bring on a rapid engagement afs the ableft general of them aw could hai started.

L. Lumb. Ay, leave them together, they'll foon come to a right underftanding, I warrant you, or the needle and the load-ftone have loft their fympathy.

[*Exit* L. Lum. *and* Sir Pert.

[*Lady* Rodolpha *ftands at that fide of the ftage where* Sir Pertinax *and* Lord Lumbercourt *went off, in amazement—Egerton is at the oppofite fide, who, after fome anxious emotions, fettles into a deep reflection.*

L. Rodol. [*Afide.*] Why this is downright tyranny. It has quite damped my speerits, and my betrothed, yonder, seems planet-struck too, I think.

Egert. [*Aside.*] A whimsical situation, mine.

L. Rodol. [*Aside.*] Ha! ha! ha! methinks we luock like a couple or cautious generals, that are obliged till take the field, but neither of us seems willing till come till action.

Egert. [*Aside.*] I protest, I know not how to address her.

L. Rodol. He weel nai advance, I fee—what am I to do in this affair? gude traith, I weel even do as I suppose many brave heroes hai done before me, clap a gude face upon the matter, and so conceal an aching heart, under a swaggering countenance. [*Aside. As she advances, she mocks and points at him, and smothers a laugh.*] Sir, as we hai, by the commands of our gude fathers, a business of some little consequence till transact, I hope you will excuse my taking the liberty of my recommending—a chair till you, for the repose of your body, in the embarrassed deliberation of your perturbed spirit.

Egert. [*Greatly embarrassed.*] Madam, I beg your pardon. [*Hands her a chair, then one for himself.*] Please to sit, madam. [*They sit down with great ceremony, she sits down first, he sits at a distance from her, silent some time, he coughs, hems, and adjusts himself, she mimics him.*]

L. Rodol. [*Aside.*] Aha, he's resolv'd not to come too near till me, I think.

Egert. [*Aside.*] A pleasant interview this—hem—hem.

L. Rodol. [*Aſide.*] Hem, he will not open the con-
greſs I ſee—then I weel. [*Very loud.*] Come, ſir !—
when will you begin ?——

Egert. [*Greatly ſurpriſed.*] Begin ! what, madam ?

L. Rodol. To make love till me.

Egert. Love, madam !

L. Rodol. Ay, love, ſir !—why you hai never ſaid
a word till me yet upon the ſubject—nor caſt a ſingle
glance at me, nor heaved one tender ſigh, nor even
ſecretly ſqueezed my loof.—Now, ſir, tho' our fathers
are ſo tyrannical, aſs to diſpoſe of us without the
conſent of our hearts, yet you, ſir, I hope, hai mair
humaneity, than to think of marrying me, without
admaniſtering ſome o' preleemeenaries uſual on
theſe occaſions, if not till my underſtanding and ſen-
timents, yet till the vanity o' my ſex at leaſt—I
hope you weel pay ſome lectle treebute of ceremony
and adulation—that, I think, I hai a right till ex-
pect.

Egert Madam, I own your reproach is juſt, I ſhall
therefore no longer diſguiſe my ſentiments, but fairly
let you know my heart.

L. Rodol. [*Starts up and runs to him.*] Ah ! ye are
right, ye are right, couſin—honeſtly and affectionately
right—that's what I like of aw things in my ſwain—
ay, ay, couſin, open your heart frankly till me, aſs a
true loover ſhould —But ſit ye down—I ſhall return
your frankneſs and your paſſion, couſin, we aw melt-
ing tenderneſs equal to the amorous enthuſiaſm of an
antient hereine.

Egert. Madam, if you will hear me.

D

L. Rodol. But remember ye muſt begin with far-
vency, and a moſt rapturous vehemence, for ye are to
conſider, couſin, that our match is nai till ariſe frai
the union of hearts, and a long decorum of ceremo-
nious courtſhip ; but is inſtantly till ſtart at yeance
out of neceſſeety or mere acceedent. Ha ! ha ! ha !
—like a match in an antient romance—where ye
ken, couſin, the knight and the damſel are mutually
ſmitten and dying for each other, at firſt ſight, or by
an amorous ſympathy, before they exchange a ſingle
glance.

Egert. Dear madam, you entirely miſtake.

L. Rodol. And our faithers, ha ! ha ! ha ! our fai-
thers are to be the dark mageecians that are till faſci-
nate our hearts, and conjure us till gether whether we
weel or not.

Egert. Ridiculous !

L. Rodol. So, noow couſſh, wi the true romantic
enthuſiaſm, ye are till ſuppoſe me the Lady o' the En-
chanted Caſtle—and ye—ha ! ha ! ha !—ye are till
be the Knight o' the ſorrowful countenance—ha ! ha!
ha !—and, upon honour, you luock the character ad-
mirably—ha ! ha ! ha !

Egert. Trifling creature !

L. Rodol. Come, ſir—why do ye no begin to raviſh
me—wi your valour, your vows, your knight-errantry,
and your amorous freazy ; nay, nay, couſin, guid ye
do no begin at yeance, the Lady o' the Enchanted
Caſtle weel vaniſh in a twinkling.

Egert. Lady Rodolpha, I know your talent for
raillery well ; but at preſent in my caſe, there is a
kind of cruelty in it.

L. Rodol. Raillery ! upon honour, coufin, ye miftake me quite and clean—I am ferious, very ferions, ay, and have caufe till be ferious—nay, I weel fubmit my cafe even till yourfelf ; [*Begins to whine*] can any poor loſſy be in a mair lamentable condition than to be fent four hundred miles by the commands of a pofitive grandmaither, till marry a man who, I find, has nai mair affection for me, than if I had been his wife thefe feven years.

Egert. Madam, I am extremely forry——

L. Rodol. But it is vary weel, coufin, vary weel— [*Cries and fobs.*] I fee your unkindnefs and averfion plain enough, and, fir, I muft tell you fairly, ye are the ainly man that ever flighted my perfon, or that drew tears fra thefe een—but it is vary weel—it's vary weel. [*Cries.*] I weel return till Scotland to-morrow morning, and let my grandmaither know how I hai been affronted by your flights, your contempts, and your averfions.

Egert. If you are ferious, madam, your diftrefs gives me a deep concern ; but affection is not in our power, and when you know that my heart is irrevocably given to another woman, I think your underftanding and good-nature, will not only pardon my paft coldnefs and neglect of you, but forgive, when I tell you, I never can have that honour which is intended me—by a connection with your ladyfhip.

L. Rodol. How, fir, are ye ferious ?

Egert. [*Rifes*] Madam, I am too deeply interefted, both as a man of honour and a lover, to act otherwife with you on fo tender a fubject.

L. Rodol. And fo you perfaft in flighting me ?—its vary weel.

Egert. I beg your pardon, madam, but I muft be explicit, and at once declare, that I never can give my hand—when I cannot give my heart.

L. Rodol. Why then, fir, I muft tell ye, that your declaration is fic an affront afs nai woman of fpeerit can, or ought to bear—and here I make a folema voow never till pardon it—but on yean condition.

Egert. If that condition be in my power, madam —

L. Rodol. Sir, it is i' your poower.

Egert. Then, madam, you may command me.

L. Rodol. Why then, fir, the condection is this, ye muft here give me your honour, that nay importunity, command, or menace o' your faither – in fine, that nai confideration whatever, fhall induce you to take me Redolpha Lumburcourt till be your wedded wife.

Egert. Madam, I moft folemnly promife, I never will.

L. Rodol. And I, fir, in my turn, moft folemnly and fincerely thank you for your refolution [*Curtfeys.*] and your agreeable averfion—ha! ha! ha! for ye hai made me as happy—afs a poor wretch reprieved in the vary inftant of intanded execution.

Egert. Pray, madam, how am I to underftand all this ?

L. Rodol. Sir, your franknefs and fincerity demand the fame behaviour on my fide—therefore, without feuther difguife or ambiguity, know, fir, that I my-

felf, am afs deeply fmitten, wi a certain fwain, afs I
underftand ye are wi your Conftantia.

Egert. Indeed, madam!

L. Rodol. O! fir, notwithftanding aw my fhew of
mirth and courage, here I ftand afs errant a trembling
Thifbe as ever fighed or mourned for her Peeramus.
O! fir, all my extravagant leveety and redeeculous be-
haviour in your prefence, noow, and ever fince your
faither prevailed on mine to confent till this match,
has been a premeditated fcheme, to provoke your gra-
vity and gude fenfe intill a cordial difguft and pofitive
refufal.

Egert. Madam, you have contrived, and acted your
fcheme moft happily.

L. Rodol. Then fince Cupid has thus luockeely dif-
pofed of ye till your Conftantia, and me till my fwain,
we hai naithing till think of noow, fir, but to contrive
hoow to reduce the inordinate paffions of oor parents
intill a temper of prudence and humanity.

Egert, Moft willingly I confent to your propofal;
but with your leave, madam, if I may prefume fo far,
pray who is your lover?

L. Rodol. Why in that too I fhall furprife you, per-
haps, mere than ever—In the firft place, he is a beg-
gar, and in difgrace wi an unforgiving faither—and
in the next place, fir, he is [*Curtfeys.*] your ain bro-
ther.

Egert. Is it poffible?

L. Rodol. A moft amorous truth, fir; that is afs
far afs a woman can anfwer for her ain heart; fo you
fee coufin Chairles, that I could nai mingle affections
we ye, I hai ne ganged oot o' the family.

Egert. Madam, give me leave to congratulate my-
felf upon your affection—you could not have placed
it on a worthier object, and whatever is to our chance
in this lottery of our parents, be affured, that my
fortune fhall be devoted to your happinefs and
his.

L. Rodol. Generous indeed, coufin, but not a whit
nobler, I affure you, than your brother Sandy be-
lieves of you; and be affured, fir, that we fhall re-
member it, while the heart feels, or memory retains
a fenfe of gratitude. But noow, fir, let me afk one
queftion—pray how is your mother affected in this bu-
finefs?

Egert. She knows of my paffion, and will, I am fure,
be a friend to the common caufe.

L. Rodol. Ah! that's lucky, our firft ftep then
muft be to take her advice in our conduct, fo as to
keep our faithers in the dark, till we can hit off fome
meafure, that wee'll wind them aboot till oor ain
purpofe, and the common intereft of our ain paffion.

Egert. You are very right, madam, for fhould my
father fufpect my brother's affection for your ladyfhip,
or mine for Conftantia, there is no guefling what would
be the confequence; his whole happinefs depends up-
on this bargain with my lord, for it gives him the pof-
feffion of three boroughs, and thofe, madam, are much
dearer to him, than the happinefs of his children; I
am forry to fay it, but to gratify his political rage, he
would facrifice every focial tie that is dear to friend or
family.   [*Exeunt.*

ACT IV. SCENE I.

Enter Sir Pertinax *and Counfellor* Plausible.

Sir Pertinax.

No—no—come away Counfellor Plaufible—come away, I fay—let them chew upon it—let them chew upon it. Why, counfellor, did you ever hear fo impartinant, fo meddling, and fo obftinate a blockhead, as that Serjeant Eitherfide ? Confound the fellow, he has put me oot of aw temper.

Plauf. He is very pofitive, indeed, Sir Pertinax, and, no doubt, was intemperate and rude--But, Sir Pertinax, I. would not break off the match notwith-ftanding ; for certainly, even without the boroughs, it is a very advantageous bargain to you, and your. fon.

Sir Pert. But zoons, Plaufible, do you think I will gee up the nomineetion till three boroughs ? Why, I would rather gee him twenty, aw thirty thoofand pounds in any either point of the bargain, efpecially at this juncture, when votes are likely to become invaluable : Why, mon, if a certain affair comes on, they'll rife above five hundred per cent.

Plauf. You judge very rightly, Sir Pertinax, but

what shall we do in this case? For Mr. Serjeant in-
sists, that you positively agreed to my lord's having
the nomination to the three boroughs, during his own
life.

Sir Pert. Why, yes, in the first sketch of the agree-
ment, I believe I did consent, but at that time, mon,
my lord's affairs did not appear to be half so desperate,
as I now find they turn oot—Sir, he must acqueese
in whatever I demand—For I hai gotten him into sic
an hobble, that he canno exeest without me.

Plauf. No doubt, Sir Pertinax, you have him abso-
lutely in your power.

Sir Pert. Vary weel, and ought not a mon to make
his vantage of it?

Plauf. No doubt you ought—no manner of doubt.
—But, Sir Pertinax, there is a secret spring in this
business, that you do not seem to perceive, and
which I am afraid, governs the matter respecting these
boroughs.

Sir Pert. What spring do you mean, counsellor?

Plauf. Why Serjeant Eitherside, I have some rea-
son to think that my lord is tied down by some means
or other to bring the serjeant in the very first vacancy
for one of those boroughs—now that I believe is the
sole motive, why the serjeant is so very strenuous, that
my lord should keep the boroughs in his own power,
fearing that you might reject him, for some man of
your own.

Sir Pert. Odds wounds, and deeth, Plausible—ye
are cleever—deevilish cleever—by the blood, ye hai
hit upon the vary streeng, that hais made aw this dif-

ACT IV.   MAN OF THE WORLD.   65

cord—I fee it—I fee it now—But haud—haud—bide
a-wee a bit—a wee bit mon—I hai a thought come in
till my head—Yas, I think noow Plaufible wee a lit-
tle care in our negociation, that this vary ftring pro-
perly tuned may be ftill made to produce the harmony
we wifh for ; yes, yes, I hai it.   This ferjeant I fee
underftonds bufinefs, and if I am not miftaken knows
how till take 'a hint.

Plauf. O ! nobody better, Sir Pertinax—nobody
better.

Sir Pert. Why then, Plaufible, the fhort road is
always the beft ; wee fic a mon ye muft even come up
to his mark at yeance, and affure him frae me, that
I weell fecure him a feat for yean of thefe vary bo-
roughs.

Plauf. O that will do, Sir Pertinax—that will do,
I'll anfwer for it.

Sir Pert. And further, I beg ye weel let him know
that I think myfelf oblig'd till confeeder him in this af-
fair afs acting for me, afs weel afs for my lord, afs a
common friend till baith, and for the fervice he has
already done us, make my fpecial compliments till
him, and pray let this amiacable bit of paper be my
faithful advocate till convince him of what my grati-
tude further intends, for his great [*Gives a bank bill.*]
equity in adjufting this agreement betwcext my lord's
family and mine.

Plauf. Ha ! ha ! ha ! Sir Pertinax, upon my word
this is noble—ay, ay, this is an eloquent bit of paper
indeed.

Sir Pert. Maifter Plaufible, in aw human dealings

the moſt effectual method is that of gauging at yeance,
till the vary bottom of a mon's heart, for if we expact
that men ſhould ſerve us, we muſt firſt win their
affections, by ſerving them—Oh, here they baith
come.

Enter Lord LUMBERCOURT, *and Serjeant* EITHER-
SIDE.

L. Lum. My dear Sir Pertinax, what could pro-
voke you to break off this buſineſs ſo abruptly? You
are really wrong in the point, and if you will give
yourſelf time to recollect, you will find that my hav-
ing the nomination to the boroughs for my life, was
a preliminary article—and I appeal to Mr. Serjeant
Eitherſide here, whether I did not always underſtand
ſo.

Serj. Either. I aſſure you, Sir Pertinax, that in all
his lordſhip's converſation with me upon this buſineſs,
and in his poſitive inſtructions, both he and I, always
underſtood the nomination to be in my lord, *durante
vita.*

Sir Pert. Why then, my lord, to ſhorten the diſpute,
all I can ſay in anſwer to your lordſhip is, that there
has been a total miſtake between us in that point, and
therefore the treaty muſt end here—I give it up—
Oh! I waſh my hands of it for ever.

Plauſ. Well, but gentlemen, gentlemen, a little pa-
tience—ſure this miſtake, ſomehow or other, may be
rectified. Mr. Serjeant, prithee let you and I ſtep
into the next room by ourſelves, and re-conſider the

claufe relative to the boroughs, and try if we cannot hit upon a medium that will be agreeable to both parties.

Serj. Either. [*With great warmth.*] Mr. Plaufible, I have confidered the claufe fully, and am entirely mafter of the queftion. My lord cannot give up the point without an equivalent.

Plauf. Sir Pertinax, will you permit Mr. Serjeant and me to retire a few moments to re-confider the points ?

Sir Pert. Wee all my heart and faul, Maifter Plaufible—ainy thing till accommodate your lordfhip, ainy thing—ainy thing.

Plauf. What fay you, my lord ?

L. Lum. Nay, I fubmit it intirely to you, and Mr. Serjeant.

Plauf. Come, Mr. Serjeant, let us retire.

L. Lum. Ay, ay, go Mr. Serjeant, and hear what Mr. Plaufible has to fay, however.

Serj. Either. Nay, I will wait on Mr. Plaufible, my lord, with all my heart, but I am fure I cannot fuggeft the fhadow of a reafon for altering my prefent opinion !—Impoffible !—Impoffible !

Plauf. Well, well, do not be pofitive, Mr. Serjeant, do not be pofitive—I am fure reafon, and your client's conveniency, will always make you alter your opinion.

Serj. Either. Ay, ay, reafon, and my client's conveniency, Mr. Plaufible, will always controul my opinion, depend upon it—Ay, ay, there you are right.— Sir, I attend you.   [*Exeunt lawyers.*

Sir Pert. I am forry, my lord, extremely forry, indeed, that this miftake has happened.

L. Lum. Upon my honour fo am I, Sir Pertinax.

Sir Pert. But come now—after all, your lordfhip muft allow ye hai been i' the wrong; come, my dear lord, you muft allow that now.

L. Lum. How fo——my dear Sir Pertinax?

Sir Pert. Not aboot the boroughs, my lord, for thofe I do not mind a bawbee, but aboot your diftruft of my friendfhip; why do you think now (I appeal to your ain breaft, my lord) do you think, my lord, that I fhould ever hai refufed, or flighted your lordfhip's nomination to thefe boroughs?

L. Lum. Why really I don't think you would, Sir Pertinax, but we muft be directed by our lawyers you know.

Sir Pert. Hah! my lord, lawyers are a dangerous fpecies of animals till hai dependance on—they are awways ftarting punctilios, and diffeecultys among friends: why, my dear lord, it is their intereft that aw mankind fhould be at variance, for difagreement is the very manure wee which they enrich and fatten the land of leeteegation, and as they find that that conftantly promotes the beft crop, depend upon it, they will awways be fure to lay it on as thick as they can.

L. Lum. Come, come, my dear Sir Pertinax, you muft not be angry with Mr. Serjeant for his infifting fo ftrongly on this point—for thofe boroughs, you know, are my fheet anchor.

Sir Pert. I know it, my lord—and as an inſtance of my promptneſs to ſtudy, and my acquieſcence till your lordſhip's inclinations, aſs 1 ſee that this Serjeant Eitherſide wiſhes you weel, and ye him, 1 think now he wou'd be as gude a mon to be returned for yean of theſe boroughs aſs could be pitched upon; and aſs ſuch, I humbly recommend him to your lordſhip's conſideration.

L. Lum. Why, my dear Sir Pertinax, to tell you the truth, I have already promiſed him—he muſt be in for one of them, and that is one reaſon why I inſiſted ſo ſtrenuouſly—He muſt be in.

Sir Pert. And why not—Odzoons ! why not ?—Is nai your word a fiat, and wall it not be always ſo to me—Are ye nai my friend—my patron—and are we nai by this match of our cheeldren, to be united intill one intereſt ?

L. Lum. So I underſtand it, I own, Sir Pertinax.

Sir Pert. My lord, it can be no otherwiſe—then, for heaven's ſake, as your lordſhip and I can have but one intereſt for the future, let us hai nai mare words aboot theſe paltry boroughs, but conclude the agreement at yeance, juſt as it ſtands, otherwiſe there muſt be new writings drawn, new conſultation of lawyers, new objections, and delays will ariſe, creditors will be impatient, and impertinant ; ſo that wee ſhall nai finiſh the Lord knows when.

L. Lum. You are right—you are right—ſay no more, Mac—ſay no more—ſplit the lawyers—you judge the point better than all Weſtminſter-hall could.

Enter Egerton.

Come hither, Charles?

Egert. Your pleasure, sir?

Sir Pert. Aboot twa hoors since I told you, Chairles, that I received this letter express, complaining of your brother's acteevety at an election i' the north, against a particular friend of mine, which has given great offence ; and, sir, ye are mentioned in the letter as well as he ; to be plain, I must roundly tell you, that upon this interview depends my happiness afs a man, and a faither, and my affection till ye, sir, as a son, for the remainder of our days.

Egert. I hope, sir, I shall never do any thing either to forfeit your affection, or disturb your happiness.

Sir Pert. I hope so too—but to the point—the fact is this—there has been a motion made, this very day, to bring on the grand affair, which is settled for Friday se'nnight.—Noow, sir, afs ye are popular, hai talents, and are weel heard, it is expected, and I insist on it, that ye endeavour till atone for your past misconduct by preparing, and taking a large share in that question, and supporting it wee aw your power.

Egert. Sir, I have always divided as you directed, except on one occasion—never voted against your friends, only in that affair, but, sir, I hope you will

not fo exert your influence, as to infift upon my fup-
porting a meafure, by an obvious proftituted fophiftry,
in direct oppofition to my character, and to my own
confcience.

Sir Pert. Confcience! Why ye are mad!—Did ye
ever hear any mon talk of confcience in poleetical
maiters?—Confcience, quotha!—I have been in Par-
liament thefe three and thraty years, and never heard
the term made ufe of before.—Sir, it is an unparlia-
mentary word, and ye weel be laughed at for it—
therefore, I defire ye wull not offer till impofe upon
me wee fuch phantoms, but let me know your reafon
for thus flighting my friends, and difobeying my com-
mands.—Sir, give me an immediate, and precife an-
fwer.

Egert Then, fir, I muft frankly tell you, that you
work againft my nature, you would connect me with
men I defpife, and prefs me into meafures I abhor,
would make me a devoted flave to felfifh leaders, who
have no friendfhip but in faction, no merit but in cor-
ruption, nor intereft in any meafure but their own,
and to fuch men I cannot fubmit.—For know, fir,
that the malignant ferment which the venal ambition
of the times provokes in the heads and hearts of other
men, I deteft.

Sir Pert. What are you aboot, fir? Malignant fer-
ment and venal ambition! every mon fhould be am-
beetious till ferve his country, and every mon fhould
be rewarded for it. And pray, fir, would ye not
weefh to ferve your country? I fay, fir, would ye not
weefh to ferve your country?

Egert. Only fhow me how I may ferve my country, and my life is her's; were I qualified to lead her armies, to fteer her fleets, and deal her honeft vengeance on her infulting foes, or could my eloquence pull down a ftate Leviathan, mighty with the plunder of his country, black with the treafons of her difgrace, and fend his infamy down to a free pofterity, as a monumental terror to corrupt ambition, I would be foremoft in fuch fervice, and act it with the unremitting ardour of a Roman fpirit.

Sir Pert. Vary weel, fir !—the fellow is befide himfelf.

Egert. But to be a common barker at envied power, to beat the drum of faction, and found the trumpet of infidious patriotifm—only to difplace a rival—or to be a fervile voter in proud corruption's filthy train, to market out my voice, my reafon, and my truft, to the party broker who beft can promife or pay for proftitution !—Thefe, fir, are fervices my nature abhors—for they are fuch a malady to every kind of virtue, as muft, in time, deftroy the faireft conftitution, that ever wifdom framed, or virtuous liberty fought for !

Sir Pert. Why ye are mad, fir !—Ye hai certainly been bit by fome mad whig or other.—Ah ! ye are vary young—vary young in thefe matters ; but experience wull convince you, fir, that every man in public bufinefs has twa confciencees, a releegious, and a poleetical confcience. Why, you fee a merchant, noow, or a fhopkeeper, or a lawyer, that kens the fcience of the world, awways luocks upon an oath in a cuftom-houfe, or behind a coounter, or in a chancery fuit, only afs an oath in bufinefs, a thing of courfe, a mere thing of courfe, that hais naithing till do wee releegion, and juft fo it is at an election——for inftance, noow—I am a candidate, pray obferve—and I gang till a perreewig-maker, a hatter, or a hofier, and I give him ten, twenty, or thraty guineas for a perreewig, hat, or a pair of hofe, fo on through a majority of votes— vary weel, what is the confequence ? Why this you fee begets a commercial intercourfe, begets friendfhip betwixt us, and in a day or two thefe men gang, and give me their fuffrages.—Noow, pray, fir, can ye or any lawyer, divine, or cafuift, caw this a bribe ? hai, fir ? in fair poleetical reafoning, it is ainly generofity on the ain fide, and gratitude on the other—So, fir, let me hai nai mair of your releegious or philofophical refinements ; but prepare, attend, and fpeak to the queftion, or ye are nai fon of mine ; fir, I infift on it.

Enter SAM.

Sam. Sir, my lord fays the writing are now ready, and his lordfhip, and the lawyers, are waiting for you and Mr. Egerton.

Sir Pert. Vary weel—we'll attend his lordfhip.— *Exit* Sam]—I tell you, Chairles, aw this confcientious refinement in poleetics, is downright ignorance, and impracticable romance ; and, fir, I defire I may hear no more of it. Come, fir, let us gang doon, and difpatch the bufinefs.   [*Going, is ftopt by* Egert.

Egert. Sir, with your permiſſion, I beg you will firſt hear me a word or two upon this ſubject.

Sir Pert. Weel, ſir, what waid ye ſay?

Egert. I have often reſolved to let you know my averſion to this match.

Sir Pert. How, ſir?

Egert. But my reſpect, and fear of diſobliging you, ſir, kept me ſilent.

Sir Pert. Your averſion!—your averſion, ſir!— How dare you uſe ſic language to me? Your averſion! Luock you, ſir, I ſhall cut the maitter ſhort— confeeder my fortune is nai inheritance, 'tis aw my ain acqueeſeetion—I can make ducks and drakes of it—ſo do not provoke me, but ſign the articles directly.

Egert. I beg your pardon, ſir, but I muſt be free on this occaſion, and tell you at once, that I can no longer diſſemble the honeſt paſſion that fills my heart for another woman.

Sir Pert. Hoow! another woman! and you villain how dare you love another woman weethout my leave? But what other woman? What is ſhe? Speak, ſir— ſpeak———

Egert. Conſtantia

Sir Pert. Conſtantia! O! ye profligate! What! a creature taken in for charity?

Egert. Her poverty is not her crime, ſir, but her misfortune. Her birth is equal to the nobleſt, and virtue, though covered with a village garb, is virtue ſtill, and of more worth to me than all the ſplendor of ermined pride, or redundant wealth, and therefore, ſir———

Sir Pert. Haud your jaubbering, ye villain!—haud your jaubbering—none of your romance, or refinement till me—I hai but yean queftion to afk ye—but yean queftion, and then hai done wee ye for ever—for ever—therefore, think before ye anfwer—Wee'll ye marry the lady? or wee'll ye break my heart?

Egert. Sir, my prefence fhall not offend you any longer—but when reafon and reflection take their turn, I am fure you will not be pleafed with yourfelf for this unpaternal paffion. [*Going away.*]

Sir Pert. Tarry, I command ye!—and I command ye likewife, not to ftir till ye hai given me an anfwer, a definitive anfwer, wull you marry the lady, or wull ye not?

Egert. Since you command me, fir, know then, that I cannot, will not marry her.   [*Exit Egert.*

Sir Pert. O! the villain has fhot me through the head!—he has cut my vitals!—I fhall run diftracted! The fellow deftroys aw my meafures—aw my fchemes—there never was fic an a bargain, afs I hai made wi this feulifh lord—poffeffion of his whole eftate, wee' three boroughs upon it—fax members—why—what an acqueefeetion?—what confequence!—what dignity!—what weight till the houfe of Mac Sycophant!—O! dom the fellow!—three boroughs, only for fending down fax broomfticks.—O! meefeerable! meefeerable! ruined! undone!—For thefe five and thraty years, fince this fellow came intill the world, I have been fecretly preparing him for the feat of minifteerial dignity; and wee the fellow's ailoquence, abeelitys, popularity, thefe boroughs, and proper connections, he might certainly in a leetle time hai done the deed.—And fure naver—naver— were times fo favourable—avery thing confpires, for aw the auld poleetical poft-horfes are broken winded, and foundered, and canno get on, and afs till the ri- fing generations, the vanity of furpaffing yean another in what they feulifhly call tafte, and ailegance, binds them hond and foot in the chains of luxury, whach wull awways fet them up till the beft beeder, fo that if they can but get wherewithall till fupply their dif. fipation, a meenifter may convert the poleetical mo- rals of aw fuch voluptuaries intill a vote that would fell the nation till Prefter John, and their boafted le- berties to the great Mogul.   And this opportunity I fhall lofe, by my fon's marrying a vartuous beggar for fove —O ! confound her vartue! it wull drive me diftracted !   [Exit.

ACT V. SCENE I.

Enter Sir PERTINAX, *and* BETTY.

Sir Pertinax.

COME this way, girl—come this way—you are a gude girl, and I'll reward you for this difcovery—O! the villain! offer her marriage!

Bet. It is true indeed, fir—I wou'd not tell your honour a lie for the world ; but, in troth, it lay upon my confcience, and I thought it my duty to tell your worfhip.

Sir Pert. Ye are right—ye are right—it was your duty to tell me, and I'll reward you for it; but, you fay, Maifter Sidney is in love we her too—Pray hoow come ye by that intelligence?

Bet. O, fir, I know when folks are in love, let them ftrive to hide it as much as they will—I know it by Mr. Sidney's eyes, when I fee him ftealing a fly fide look at her—by his trembling—his breathing fhort—-his fighing when they are reading together ; befides, fir, he made love verfes upon her in praife of her virtue, and her playing upon the mufic—Ay, and I fufpect another thing, fir—-fhe has a fweet-heart if not a hufband, not far from hence. .

Sir Pert. Wha ! Conftantia !

Bet. Ay, Conftantia, fir—Lord, I can know the whole affair, fir, only for fending over to Hadley, to farmer Hilford's, youngeft daughter, Sukey Hilford.

Sir Pert. Then fend this minute, and get me a particular account of it.

Bet. That I will, fir.

Sir Pert. In the mean time, keep a ftrict watch upon Conftantia, and be fure you bring me word of whatever new maiter ye can pick up aboot her, my fon, or this Hadley hufband, or fweet-heart

Bet. Never fear, fir.   [*Exit Betty.*

Sir Pert. This love of Sidney's, for Conftantia, is not unlikely—there is fomething promifing in it—yas, I think it is nai impoffible till convert it intill a fpecial and immediate advantage—it is but trying—Wha's there ?—if it miffes, I am but where I was.

Enter TOMLINS.

Where is maifter Sidney ?

Tom. In the drawing room, fir.

Sir Pert. Tell him I would fpeak with him—[*Exit Tomlins.*]—'Tis more than probable—fpare till fpake, and fpare till fpeed—try—try—awways try the human heart—try is as gude a maxim in poleetics as in war.—Why, fuppofe this Sidney noow, fhould be privy to his friend Chairles's love for Conftantia—what then ?—gude traith it is natural till think, that his ain love will demand the preference—ay, obtain it too—yas, yas, felf—felf is an ailoquent advocate on thefe occafions, and feldom lofes his caufe. I hai the general preenciple o' human nature at leaft till encourage me in the expcreement, for only make it a mon's intereft till be a rafcal, and I think we may fafely depend upon his integreety in ferving himfelf.

Enter SIDNEY.

Sid. Sir Pertinax, your fervant—Mr. Tomlins told me you defired to fpeak with me.

Sir Pert. Yas, I wanted till fpeak to ye, upon a vary fingular bufinefs—Maifter Sidney, gi me your hand—guin it did not luook like flattery, which I deteft, I would tell ye, Maifter Sidney, that ye are an honour till your cloth, your country, and till human nature.

Sid. You are very obliging.

Sir Pert. Sit ye doon here, Maifter Sidney—fit ye doon by me, my friend, I am under the greateft obligations till ye, for the care ye have taken of Chairles—the preenceeples, releegious, moral, and polectical, that ye hai infufed intill him, demand the warmeft return of gratitude, baith frai him, and frai me.

Sid. Your approbation, fir, next to that of my own confcience, is the beft teft of my endeavours, and the higheft applaufe they can receive.

Sir Pert. Sir, ye deferve – richly deferve it—and noow, fir, the fame care that ye hai had of Chairles,

E

the fame my wife hai taken of her favourite Conftantia, and fure never were accomplifhments, knowledge, or preenciples, focial and releegious, infufed into a better nature than Conftantia.

Sid. In truth, fir, I think fo too.

Sir Pert. She is befides, a gentlewoman of afs good a family afs any o' this country.

Sid. So I underftand, fir.

Sir Pert. Her father had a vaft eftate, which he diffipated and melted in feaftings, and friendfhips, and chareeties, and hofpitalities, and fic kind of nonfenfe —but the bufinefs, Maifter Sidney—I love ye, yas, I love ye, and hai been luocking oot, and contriving hoow till fettle ye in the world. Sir, I want to fee you comfortably and honourably fixed at the head of a refpeɛtable family, and guin ye were my ain fon a thoofand times, I could nai make a mair valuable prefent till ye for that purpofe, afs a pairtner for life, than this fame Conftantia, wi fic a fortune doown we her, afs ye yourfel fhall deem till be competent; ay, and an affurance of every canonical conteengency in my poower till corfer or promote.

Sid. Sir, your offer is noble and friendly; but tho' the higheft ftation would derive luftre from Conftantia's charms and worth; yet, were fhe more amiable than love cou'd paint her in the lover's fancy, and wealthy beyond the thirft of mifers appetite, I cou'd not—wou'd not wed her!—[*Rifes.*]

Sir Pert. Not wed her! Qdfwins mon, ye furprife me! why fo, what hinders?

Sid. I beg you will not afk a reafon for my refufal

—but briefly and finally it cannot be—nor is it a fubject I can talk longer upon.

Sir Pert. Weel, fir, I hai done—I hai done—fit doon mon—fit doon again, fit ye doon—I fhall mention it no more—not but I muft confefs honeftly till ye, friend Sidney, that the match, had ye approved of my propofal, befides profiting ye, would have been of fingular fervice till me likewife ; however, ye may ftill ferve me afs effectually afs if ye had married her.

Sid. Then, fir, I am fure I will moft heartily.

Sir Pert. I believe it, I believe it, friend Sidney, and I thank ye—I hai nai friend till depend upon but —yourfel—my heart is awmoft broke—I canno help thefe tears, and to tell ye the fact at yeance, your friend, Chairles, is ftruck we a moft dangerous malady—a kind of infanity—and ye fee I canno help weeping when I think of it.—In fhort, this Conftantia, I am afraid has caft an evil eye upon him—do ye underftond me ?

Sid. Not very well, fir.

Sir Pert. Why he is grievoufly fmitten wi the love o' her, and I am afraid will never be cured without a leetle of your affeeftance.

Sid. Of my affiftance, pray, fir, in what manner ?

Sir Pert. In what mainner ! Lord, Maifter Sidney, why hoow can ye be fo dull, why hoow is any mon cured of his love till a wench, but by ganging till bed till her—Now do you underftond me ?

Sid. Perfectly, fir—perfectly.

Sir Pert. Gude friend, guin ye wou'd but gai him that hint, and take an opportunity till fpake a gude

word for him, till the wench, and guin ye would like-
wife caft aboot a leetle now, and contrive till bring
them together once—why in a few days after he would
nai care a pinch of fnuff for her.—[*Sidney ftarts.*]
What is the maitter we you mon? What the deevil
gars ye ftart and look fo aftonifhed?

Sid. Sir, you amaze me!—In what part of my
mind or conduct have you found that bafenefs, which
intitles you to treat me with this indignity?

Sir Pert. Indignity! wha' indignity do ye mean,
fir?—is afking ye till ferve a friend we a wench an
indignity?—Sir, am not I your patron and benefactor?
Ha——

Sid. You are, fir, and I feel your bounty at my
heart, but the virtuous gratitude that fowed the deep
fenfe of it there, does not inform me in return, that
the tutor's facred function, or the focial virtue of the
man, muft be debafed into the pupil's pander, or the
patron's proftitution.

Sir Pert. Hoow! what, fir, d'ye difpute?—are ye
nai my dependant? ha! and do you hefitate aboot
an ordinary civility, which is practees'd every day, by
men and women of the firft fafhion, fir—fir, let me
tell ye, however nice ye may be—there's nai a client
aboot the court that wou'd nai jump at fic an oppor-
tunity till oblige his patron.

Sid. Indeed, fir, I believe the doctrine of pimping
for patrons, as well as that of proftituting eloquence
and public truft for private lucre may be learned in
your party fchools; for when faction and public vena-
lity are taught as meafures neceffary to good govern-

ment and general profperity, there every vice is to be
expected.

Sir Pert. O ho! O ho!—vary weel—vary weel!---
fine flander upon meenifters—fine feduction againft
government—O! ye villain---ye---ye---ye are a black
fheep, and I'll mark ye—I am glad ye fhew yourfel---
yas—yas—ye hai taken off the mafk at laft—ye hai
been in my fervice for many years, and I never ken-
ned your principles before.

Sid. Sir, you never affronted them before—if you
had, you fhou'd have—have—known them fooner.

Sir Pert. It's vary weel, I hai done wi ye—ay, ay
noow I can account for my fon's conduct, his aver-
fion till courts, till meenifters, levees, public bufinefs,
and his deefobedience till my commands.---Ah, ye
are a Judas!---a perfeedious Judas!—ye hai ruined
the morals of my fon, ye villain, but I hai done we ye
—however this I will prophecy at our pairting for
your comfort--that guin you are fo vary fqueamifh
aboot bringing a lad and a lafs together, or aboot do-
ing fic an harmlefs innocent job for your patron, you'll
never rife in the church.

Sid. Tho' my conduct, fir, fhou'd not make me
rife in her power, I am fure it will in her favour—in
the favour of my own confcience too, and in the
efteem of all worthy men! and that, fir, is a power
and dignity beyond what patrons or any minifter can
confer.   [*Exit Sidney.*

Sir Pert. What a reegorous, faucy, ftiff neck'd
rafcal it is—I fee my folly now---I am undone by my
ain policy; this Sidney was the laft mon that fhould

hai been aboot my fon—the fellow, indeed, hath given
him preenciples that might hai done vary weel among
the ancient Romans, but are damn'd unfit for the mo-
dern Breetons.—Weel, guin I had a thoofand fons, I
never wou'd fuffer yeane of your univerfity bred fel-
lows till be aboot a fon of mine again, for they hai fic
an a pride of leeterature, and character, and fic faucy
Englifh notion of leeberty continually fermenting in
their thoughts, that a mon is never fure of them till
he's a Beefhop.   Now if I had a Frenchmon or a
foreigner of any kind aboot my fon, I could hai preffed
him at yance untill my purpofe, or hai kick'd the raf-
cal oot of my houfe in a twinkling—but what am I to
do? Zounds, he muft nai marry this beggar, I cannot
fit doon tamely under that—ftay—haud—a wee, by the
blood I have it—yas, I hai hit upon 't, I'll hai the
wench fmuggled till the Highlands of Scotland to-
morrow morning—yas—yas--I'll hai her fmuggled.

Enter BITTY.

Bet. O! fir, I have got the whole fecret out!

Sir Pert. Aboot what?——

Bet. About Mifs Conftantia, I have juft had all
the particulars from farmer Hilford's youngeft daugh-
ter—Sukey Hilford!

Sir Pert. Weel, weel, but what is the ftory?
Quick, quick, what is it?

Bet. Why, fir, it is certain, that Mrs. Conftantia
has a fweetheart or a hufband, a fort of a gentleman,

or gentleman's gentleman, they don't know which, that lodges at Gaffer Hodges's, and it is whifpered all about the village, that fhe is with child by him, for Sukey fays, fhe faw them together laft night in the dark walk, and Mrs. Conftantia was all in tears.

Sir Pert. Zoonds! I am afraid this is too gude news to be true.

Bet. O! fir, it is certainly true, for I myfelf have obferved, that fhe has looked very pale for fome time, and could not eat, and has qualms every hour of the day—yes, yes, fir, depend upon it, fhe is breeding, as fure as my name is Betty Hint—befides, fir, fhe has juft written a letter to the gallant, and I have fent John the gardener to her, who is to carry it to him to Hadley.—Now, fir, if your worfhip wou'd feize it— fee—fee—here John comes with the letter in his hand.

Sir Pert. Step you oot Betty, and leave the fellow to me.

Bet. I will, fir.   [*Exit Betty.*

Enter JOHN, *with a Packet and Letter.*

John. There you go into my pocket, [*puts up the packet*] there's nobody in the library, fo I'll e'en go thro' the fhort way—Let me fee, what is the name? Mel—Meltill—O! no, Melville, at Gaffer Hodge's.

Sir Pert. What letter is that, fir?

John. Letter, fir!

Sir Pert. Give it me.

John. An pleafe you, fir, it is not mine.

Sir Pert. Deliver it this inftant, firrah, or I'll break your head.

John. There, there, your honour. [*Gives the letter to Sir Pertinax.*]

Sir Pert. Begone, rafcal—this, I fuppofe, wull let us intill the whole bufinefs.—

John. [*Afide.*] You have got the letter old furly, but the paquet is fafe in my pocket. I'll go and deliver that however ; for I will be true to poor Mrs. Conftantia, in fpite of you.   [*Exit John.*

Sir Pert. [*Reads*] Um, um, " And blefs my eyes with the fight of you ;" um, um, " throw myfelf into your dear arms"—Zounds this letter is invaluable! ah! ah! Madam—yas this will do—this will do I think—let me fee how it is directed—*To Mr. Melville* —vary weel.

Enter BETTY.

O! Betty, you are an excellent wench—this letter is worth a million.

Bet. It is as I fufpected, fir, to her gallant?

Sir Pert. It is, it is—bid Conftantia pack oot of the houfe this inftant—and let them get the chaife ready to carry her where fhe pleafes—but firft; fend my wife and fon hither.

Bet. I fhall, fir.

Sir Pert. Do fo—begone. [*Exit Betty.*] Aha! Maifter Chairles, I believe I fhall cure you of your

paſſion for a beggar noow---I think he canno be ſo in-
fatuated as till be a dupe till a detected ſtrumpet---
Let me ſee hoow am I till act noow? why, like a true
poleetician, I muſt pretend moſt ſincerity, when I in-
tend moſt decei⸫ ——

Enter Lady MAC SYCOPHANT, *and* EGERTON.

, Weel, Chairles, notwithſtanding the meeſery ye hai
brought upon me, I hai ſent for ye and your meither,
in order to convince ye baith of my affection, and my
readineſs till forgive, nay, and even till indulge your
perverſe paſſion ; for ſince I find this Conſtantia has
got hold of your heart, and that your meither and ye
think, that ye can never be happy without her, why
I'll nai longer oppoſe your inclinations.

Egert. Dear ſir, you ſnatch me from the ſharpeſt
miſery—on my knees, let my heart thank you for this
goodneſs.

L. Mac. Let me expreſs my thanks too---and my
joy---for had you not conſented to his marriage here,
we all ſhould have been miſerable.

Sir Pert. Weel, I am glad I hai found a way till
pleaſe ye baith at laſt---but my dear Chairles, [*With
paternal tenderneſs.*] ſuppoſe noow, that this ſpotleſs
veſtal, this wonder of vartue---this idol of your heart,
ſhou'd be a conceal'd wanton after aw !

Egert. A wanton, ſir !

Sir Pert. Or ſhou'd have an engagement of mar-
riage, or an intrigue wi another mon, and is only

making a dupe of ye aw this time—I say, only sup-
pose it, Chairles, what would become ye think of
her ?

Egert. I shou'd think her the most deep, deceitful,
and most subtil of her sex, and if possible, wou'd ne-
ver think of her again.

Sir Pert. Wi ye gi me your honor o' that ?

Egert. Most solemnly, sir.

Sir Pert. Enough—I am satisfied—you make me
young again—your prudence has brought tears of joy
frai my very vitals—I was afraid ye were faceenated
wee the charms of a crack—do you ken this hond ?

Egert. Mighty well, sir.

Sir Pert. And ye, madam ?

L. Mac. As well as I do my own, sir—it is Con-
stantia's.

Sir Pert. It is so, and a better evidence it is than
any that can be given by the human tongue—here is a
warm, rapturous, lascivious letter, under the hypocri-
tical syren's ain hond, sir.

Egert. Pray, sir, let us hear it.

Sir Pert. Yas, yas, ye shall hear it—Eloeesa never
writ a warmer, nor a ranker till her Abelard—but
judge yourselves.

[*Egerton reads.*] " *I have only time to tell you,
that the family came down sooner than I expected, and
that I cannot bless my eyes with the sight of you till even-
ing, for my heart has no room for any wish or for-
tune, but what contributes to your relief and happi-
ness.*

Sir Pert. O! Chairles! Chairles!—Do you see, sir,

what a dupe fhe makes of ye?---but mark what fol-
lows————

[Egerton *reads.*] " *O! how I long to throw my-
felf into your dear, dear, arms, to footh your fears,
your apprehenfions, and your forrows---I have fomething
to tell you of the utmoft moment, but will referve it till we
meet this evening in the dark walk.*

Sir Pert. In the dark walk! in the dark walk!---
Ah! an evil-eyed curfe upon her!---yas, yas, fhe has
been often i' the dark walk, I believe---but lifb---
lift——

[Egerton *reads.*] " *In the mean time, banifh all fears,
and hope the beft fortune, your ever dutiful*

Conftantia Harrington."

Sir Pert. There's---there's a warm epiftle for ye---
in fhort, the huffey, ye muft know, is married till the
fellow.

Egert. Not unlikely, fir.

L. Mac. Indeed, by her letter, I believe fhe is.

Sir Pert. Nay, I know fhe is---Now, madam,
what amends can ye make me for countenancing your
fon's paffion for fic an a huffey? And ye, fir, what
ha ye till fay for your difobedience and your fren-
zy?---O! Chairles, Chairles, ye'll fhorten my
days!

Egert. Pray, fir, be patient---compofe yourfelf a
moment---I will make you any compenfation in my
power.

Sir Pert. Then inftantly fign the articles of mar-
riage.

Egert. The lady, fir, has never yet been confult-ed; and I have some reason to believe that her heart is engaged to another man.

Sir Pert. Sir, that is nai business of yours—I know she will consent, and that's all we are till consider. O! here comes my lord.

Enter Lord LUMBERCOURT.

L. Lum. Sir Pertinax, every thing is ready, the lawyers wait for us.

Sir Pert. We obey your lordship—where is Lady Rodolpha?

L. Lum. Giving some female consolation to poor Constantia. Why, my lady, ha! ha! ha! I hear your vestal, Constantia, has been flirting.

Sir Pert. Yas, yas, my lord, she is in vary gude order for ainy mon that wants a wife, and an heir till his estate into the bargain.

Enter FOOTMAN.

Foot. Sir, there's a man below that wants to speak to your honour upon particular business.

Sir Pert. Sir, I canno speak till any body noow—he must come another time—haud--Stay—Is he a gentleman?

Foot. He looks something like one, sir—a sort of a gentleman---he seems to be a kind of a gentleman, but he seems to be in a kind of a passion, for when I asked his name, he anfwered haftily —'tis no matter friend —go tell your mafter, there's a gentleman here that muft fpeak to him directly.

Sir Pert. Muft! hah! vary peremptory indeed! pray thee, let's fee him for curiofity fake.

[*Exit Footman.*

Enter Lady RODOLPHA.

L. Rodol. O! my Lady Mac Sycophant, I am come an humble advocate for a weeping piece of female frailty; who begs fhe may be permitted till fpeak till your ládyfhip before ye finally reprobate her.

Sir Pert. I beg your pardon, Lady Rodolpha—but it muft not be, fee her fhe fhall not.

L. Mac. Nay, there be no harm, my dear, in hearing what fhe has to fay for herfelf.

Sir Pert. I tell ye it fhall not be.

L. Mac. Well, well, my dear, I have done.

Enter FOOTMAN *and* MELVILLE.

Foot. Sir, that is my mafter.

Sir Pert. Weel, fir, what is your urgent bufeenefs wi me?

Mel. To fhun difgrace, and punifh bafenefs.

Sir Pert. Punifh bafenefs! what does the fellow mean? what are ye, fir?

Mel. A man, fir!—and one whofe fortune once bore as proud a fway as any within this country's limits.

L. Lum. You feem to be a foldier, fir.

Mel. I was, fir, and have the foldier's certificate to prove my fervice, rags and fcars—in my heart for ten long years, in India's parching clime, I bore my country's caufe, and in the nobleft dangers fuftained it with my fword; at length ungrateful peace has laid me down, where welcome war firft took me up—in poverty, and the dread of cruel creditors—paternal affection brought me to my native land, in queft of an only child—I found her, as I thought, amiable as parental fondnefs could defire—but luft and foul feduction, have fnatched her from me—and hither am I come, fraught with a father's anger, and a foldier's honour, to feek the feducer, and glut revenge.

L. Mac. Pray, fir, who is your daughter?

Mel. I blufh to own her—but—Conftantia.

Egert. Is Conftantia your daughter, fir?

Mel. She is—and was the only comfort that nature, or my own extravagancies had left me.

Sir Pert. Gude traith then, I fancy ye will find but vary little comfort frai her; for fhe is nai better than fhe fhou'd be—fhe has had nai damage in this manfion—I am told fhe is wi bairn—but ye may gang till Hadley, till yeane farmer Hodge's, and there ye may learn the whole ftory, and wha the faither of her bairn is, frai a cheel they call Melville.

Mel. Melville!——

Sir Pert. Yees, fir, Melville.

Mel. O! would to heaven fhe had no crime to an-
fwer, but her commerce with Melville. No, fir, he
is not the man—it is your fon, your Egerton, that
has feduced her, and here, fir, is the evidence of his
feduction.   [*Shewing the jewels.*]

Egert. Of my feduction, fir!

Mel. Of yours, if your name be Egerton!

Egert. I am that man, fir, but pray what is your evi-
dence?

Mel. Thefe bills, and thefe gorgeous jewels, not to
be had in her menial ftate, but at the price of chafti-
ty—not an hour fince fhe fent them, impudently fent
them, by a fervant of this houfe—Contagious infamy
ftarted from their touch!

Egert. Sir, perhaps you may be miftaken concern-
ing the terms on which fhe received them—do you but
clear her conduct with Melville, and I will inftantly
fatisfy your fears concerning the jewels and her vir-
tue.

Mel. Sir, you give me new life—you are my better
angel—I believe—I believe in your words—your looks
—know then, I am that Melville.

Sir Pert. Hoow, fir—ye that Melville?—that was at
farmer Hodge's?

Mel. The fame, fir. It was he brought my Con-
ftantia to my arms—lodged and fecreted me—once
my lowly tenant, now my only friend; the fear of in-
exorable creditors made me change my name from
Harrington to Melville—till I cou'd fee, and confult
fome, who once called themfelves my friends.

Egert. Sir, fufpend your fears and anger but for a few minutes, I will keep my word with you religioufly, and bring your Conftantia to your arms, as virtuous, and as happy as you cou'd wifh her.

                   [*Exit Lady* Mac *and* Egerton.

Sir Pert. [*Afide.*] The clearing up this wanch's vartue is damn'd unlooky ! I am afraid it will ruin aw oor affairs again ; however, I hai yean ftroke ftill in my head, that will fecure the bargain wi my lord, let maiters gang as they weell.—But, I wonder Maifter Melville, that ye did nai pick up fome leetle maiter of filler in the Indies—ah! there hai been bonny fortunes fnapt up there of late years, by fome of the meeleeta-ry blades.

Mel. It is very true, fir, but it is an obfervation among foldiers, that there are fome men who never meet with any thing in the fervice but blows and ill-fortune—I was one of thofe, even to a proverb.

Sir Pert. Ah ! 'tis a pity, fir, a great pity noow, that ye did nai get a mogul, or fome fic an animal in-till your clutches.—Ah ! I fhould like till hä the ftrangling of a nabob—the rummaging of his gold duft, his jewel clofet, and aw his magazines of bars and ingots—ha ! ha ! ha !—gude traith noo fic an a fellow would be a bonny cheel to bring over till this toown, and to exheebit him riding on an elephant—pon honour, a mon might raife a poll-tax by him, that woul gang near to pay the debts of the nation.

Enter EGERTON, CONSTANTIA, *Lady* MAC SYCO-
PHANT, *and* SIDNEY.

Egert. Sir, I promifed to fatisfy your fears concern-
ing your daughter's virtue, and my beft proof to you,
and all the world, that I think her not only chafte,
but the moft deferving of her fex, is, that I have made
her the partner of my heart, and tender guardian of
my earthly happinefs for life.

Sir Pert. How, married?

Egert. I know, fir, at prefent, we fhall meet your
anger, but time, reflection, and our dutiful conduct,
we hope, will reconcile you to our happinefs.

Sir Pert. Naver, naver---and cou'd I make ye, her,
and aw your iffue beggars, I wou'd move hell, hea-
ven, and earth till do it!

L. Lum. Why, Sir Pertinax, this is a total revo-
lution, and will intirely ruin all my affairs.

Sir Pert. My lord, wi the confent of your lordfhip,
and Lady Rodolpha, I hai an expedient till offer,
that will not ainly punifh that rebellious villain, but
anfwer every end that your lordfhip, and the lady pro-
pofed wi him.

L. Lum. I doubt it much, Sir Pertinax, I doubt it
much.   But what is it, fir?   What is your expedi-
ent?

Sir Pert. My lord, I hai another fon, (Sandy)
a gude lad he is---and provided the lady and your
lordfhip hai no objection till him, every article of
that rebel's intended marriage fhall be amply fulfill-

ed upon Lady Rodolpha's union with my younger
son.

L. Lum. Why that is an expedient, Sir Pertinax,
but what say you, Rodolpha?

L. Rodol. Nay, nay, my lord, afs I had nai reafon
till have the leaft affection till my coufin Egerton, and
afs my intended marriage wi him was intirely an act
of obedience till my grandmaither, provided my cou-
fin Sandy will be afs agreeable till her ladyfhip, afs
my coufin Chairles here wou'd hai been---I hai nai
the leaft objection till the change---ay, ay, upon
honour, yean brother is afs gude till Rodolpha afs an-
other.

Sir Pert. I'll anfwer, madam, for your grandmaither
---noow, my lord, what fay you?

L. Lum. Nay, Sir Pertinax, fo the agreement
ftands, all is right again. Come, child, let us be gone,
ay, ay, fo my affairs are made eafy, it is equal to me
who fhe marries---Sir Pertinax, let them be but eafy,
and rat me if I care if fhe incorporates with the Cham
of Tartary!　　　　　　[*Exit L.* Lumbercourt.

Sir Pert. As to ye, my Lady Mac Sycophant, I
fuppofe ye concluded before ye gave yer confent till
this match, that there would be an end to every thing
betwixt ye and me. Live wee your Conftantia, ma-
dam, your fon, and that black fheep there; live wee
them, ye fhall hai a jointure, but not a bawbee be-
fides, living or dead fhall ye, or any of your iffue,
ever fee of mine---and fo my vengeance light upon ye
aw together!　　　　　　[*Exit Sir* Pertinax.

L. Rodol. Weel, coufin Egerton, in fpite of the
ambeetious frenzy of yer faither, and the thoughtlefs

diffipation of mine, Don Cupid hais at laft carried his point in favour of his devotees—but I muft noow take my leave—Lady Mac Sycophant, your moft obe-dient—Maifter Sidney, yours—Permit me, Conftan-tia, till hai the honour of congratulating myfel upon oor alliance.

Con. Madam, I fhall ftudy to deferve and to return this kindnefs.

L. Rodol. I am fure you weel; but I negleĉt my poor Saundy aw this while—and gude traith, my ain heart begins to tell me what his heart feels, and chides me for tarrying fo long; I will therefore fly till him on the wings of love and good news, for I am fure the poor lad is pining wi the pip of defire, and anxious jeopardy —and fo, gude folks, I will leave ye wee the fag end of an auld north country wifh— May mutual love and gude humour be the guefts of your hearts, the theme of your tongues, and the blythfome fubjeĉt of aw your triefey dreams, thro' the rugged road of this deceitful world;—and may oor faithers be an example to oorfels, to treat oor bairns better than they hai treated us.

[*Exit Lady* Rodolpha.

Egert You feem melancholy, fir.

Mel. Thefe precarious turns of fortune, fir, will prefs upon the heart, for notwithftanding my Conftan-tia's happinefs, and mine in her's, I own, I cannot help feeling fome regret, that my misfortunes fhould be the caufe of any difagreement between a father and the man, to whom I am under the moft endearing ob-ligations.

Egert. You have no fhare in this difagreement---

for had not you been born, from my father's nature,
some other cause of his resentment must have happen'd ; --but for a time, sir, at least, and I hope for
life, afflictions, and angry vicissitudes have taken their
leave of us all. If affluence can procure content and
ease, they are within our reach---my fortune is ample,
and shall be dedicated to the happiness of this domestic circle.

My scheme, tho' mock'd by knave, coquet and fool,
To thinking minds must prove this golden rule ;
In all pursuits, but chiefly in a wife,
Not wealth, but morals, make the happy life.

F I N I S.

THE

TRUE-BORN IRISHMAN;

OR,

IRISH FINE LADY.

A

COMEDY.

BY CHARLES MACKLIN, ESQ.

THEATRICAL REPRESENTATION.

AS PERFORMED AT THE

THEATRES-ROYAL,

DRURY-LANE, COVENT-GARDEN, AND
SMOCK-ALLEY.

REGULATED FROM THE PROMPT-BOOKS,

By Permiſſion of the Managers.

"The Lines diſtinguiſhed by inverted Commas, are omitted in the Repreſentation."

DUBLIN:

PRINTED BY GRAISBERRY AND CAMPBELL,
FOR WILLIAM JONES, NO. 86, DAME-STREET.
M DCC XCIII.

M E N.

MURROGH O'DOGHERTY.
COUNT MUSHROOM.
COUNSELLOR HAMILTON.
MAJOR GAMBLE.
PAT FITZMUNGREL.
JAMES.
JOHN.
WILLIAM.

W O M E N.

MRS. DIGGERTY.
LADY KINNEGAD.
LADY BAB FRIGHTFUL.
MRS. GAZETTE.
MRS. JOLLY.
KATTY FARREL.

SCENE, Dublin.—A Room in Mr. O'Dogherty's House.

TIME—From Noon to Evening.

TRUE-BORN IRISHMAN.

ACT I. SCENE I.

Enter O'DOGHERTY *and* SERVANT.

O'Dogherty.

WHO's there?

Serv. Sir.

O'Dogh. Is John come in yet?

Serv. No, fir.

O'Dogh. Be fure fend him to me as foon as he comes in.   [*Exit* Ser.

Enter JOHN.

John. I am here, fir.

O'Dogh. Well, John, how is my brother after his journey?

F

John. The counsellor gives his compliments to you, fir, and thanks you for your enquiry: He is very well, and will wait on you as foon as he is dreſſed.

O'Dogh. Mighty well—what is that you. have in your hand, John?

John. It is nothing for you, fir---it is a card for my miſtreſs, from Madam Mulroony ; her man gave it me as I came in.

O'Dogh. Pray, let me fee it---" Mrs Mulroony makes her compliments to Mrs. Murrogh O'Dogherty, and likewife to Mr. Murrogh O'Dogherty, and hopes to have the favour of their company on Sunday the 17th inſtant, to play at cards, fup, and fpend the evening, with Lady Kinnegad, Mrs. Cardmark, Miſs Brag, Mr. Mufhroom, Cornet Bafilifk, Sir Anthony All-night, Major Gamble, and a very jolly party."—Here, John, take it to your miſtreſs—I have nothing to fay to it. [*Exit* John.]--Well done Mrs. Mulroony—faith, and it well becomes your father's daughter, and your hufband's wife, to play at cards upon a Sunday. She is another of the fine ladies of this country, who, like my wife, is fending her foul to the devil, and her hufband to a gaol as faſt as fhe can. The booby has fcarce a thoufand pounds a year in the world, yet he fpends above two thoufand in equipage; taſte, high life, and jolly parties---befides what his fool of a wife lofes to that female fharper, my Lady Kinnegad and her jolly party ; which, if I may judge by my own wife, is at leaſt a good two thoufand more ; fo that by the rule of fubtraction, take four thoufand pounds a year out of one, and in a very little time nothing will remain but a gaol, or an efcape in the packet on Connought Monday.

Enter WILLIAM *fhewing in Counfellor* HAMILTON.

Will. Counfellor Hamilton. [*Exit* Will.

O'Dogh. Counfellor, you are welcome to Dublin.

Counf. Brother, I am extremely glad to fee you.

O'Dogh. By my faith, and fo am I you. Odzooks give us a kifs, man : I give you my honour I am as glad to fee you in Dublin at this juncture, as I fhould to fee a hundred head of fat bullocks upon my own land, all ready for Ballinafloe fair.

Counf. Sir, your humble fervant. That is a great compliment from you, brother, I know.

O'Dogh. It is a very true one I affure you.

Counf. Well, I fee by the newfpapers that my fifter is returned from her coronation frolic, and in health I fuppofe, or you would have wrote me word had it been otherwife.

O'Dogh. Yes, yes, fhe is in health indeed, and returned with a vengeance.

Counf. Pray what is the matter ?

O'Dogh. Ogho ! enough is the matter, the devil an inhabitant in Swift's Hofpital for Lunatics, is in a worfe pickle than fhe is.

Counf. You furprife me !——in what refpect, pray ?

O'Dogh. Why, with a diftemper that fhe has brought over with her from England, which will, in a little time, I am afraid, infect the whole nation.

Counf. Pray, what may that be ?

O'Dogh. Sir, it is called the Irifh Fine Lady's delirium, or the London vertigo; if you were to hear her when the fit is upon her—oh, fhe is as mad—the devil a thing in this poor country but what gives her the fpleen and the vapours—then fuch a phrenzy of admiration for every thing in England—and, among the reft of her madnefs, fhe has brought over a new language with her.

Counf. What do you mean by a new language?

O'Dogh. Why a new kind of a London Englifh, that's no more like our Irifh Englifh, than a coxcomb's fine gilded chariot like a Glaffmanogue noddy. —Why what name do you think fhe went by when fhe was in England ?

Counf. Why, what name dare fhe go by but Dogherty ?

O'Dogh. Dogherty!—ogho—upon my honour fhe ftartles when fhe hears the name of Dogherty, and blufhes, and is as much afhamed as if a man had fpoke bawdy to her.—No, no, my dear, fhe is no longer the plain, modeft, good-natured, domeftic, obedient Irifh Mrs. O'Dogherty, but the travelled, rampant, high-lif'd, prancing Englifh Mrs. Diggerty.

Counf. Ha, ha, ha! Mrs. Diggerty! ridiculous!

O'Dogh. Ay, ridiculous indeed! to change her name--was there ever such impertinence? But do you know, brother, among the rest of your sister's whims and madnesses, that she is turned a great politician too concerning my name.

Counf. Ha, ha, ha! a politician!--Why how in the name of wonder and common sense can politics and the name of Dogherty be connected?

O'Dogh. O it's a wonder indeed!--but strange as it is, they are connected--but very ridiculously as you may imagine.

Counf. But, prithee, by what means?

O'Dogh. Why, you must know, we are to have an election shortly for the county that I live in, which young Lord Turnabout wants to carry for one of his own gang; and as the election in a great measure depends upon my interest, the young fox, knowing the conceit and vanity of my wife, has taken her by her favourite foible, and tickled it up, by telling her that if I direct my interest properly, it would not be difficult to procure me a title. Now, sir, this piece of flattery has stirred up such a rage of quality and title in her giddy head, that I cannot rest night or day for her importunity—in short, she would have me desert my friends, and sell myself, my honour, and my country, as several others have done before me, merely for a title, only that she may take place of a parcel of foolish idle women, and sink the antient name of Dogherty in the upstart title of Lady.

Thingum, my Lady Fiddle Faddle, or some such ridiculous nonsense.

Counf. But, sir, pray pause a little upon this business—my sister's vanity, I grant you, may be ridiculous—but though you despise titles and ostentation, yet, as your interest can certainly make the member, were I in your circumstances, I would have a voice in the senate of my country—go into parliament for the county yourself.

O'Dogh. Ogh, I have been among them already, and I know them all very well. What signifies my sitting among hundreds of people with my single opinion all alone.. When I was there before I was stigmatized as a singular blockhead, an impracticable fellow, only because I would not consent to sit like an image, and when the master of the puppets pulled the string of my jaw on one side, to say aye, and on t'other side, to say no, and to leap over a stick backwards and forwards, just as the faction of party and jobbers, and leaders, and political adventurers directed—ah, brother, brother, I have done with them all—oh, I have done with them all.

Counf. What, and after all your expence of opposing government right or wrong, and supporting your patriots, will you give them all up?

O'Dogh. Indeed I will—I was patriot mad I own, like a great many other fools in this distracted country—sir, I was so mad that I hated the very name of a courtier as much as an illiterate lay-swaddling methodist does that of a regular clergyman. But I am cured of that folly ; for now I find that a courtier is juft as honeft a man as a patriot—my dear, they are both made of the fame ftuff; ah, I have at laft found out what fort of an animal a patriot is.

Counf. Ay!—and pray, brother, what fort of an animal is he?

O'Dogh. Why he is a fort of a political weather-cock, that is blown about by every wind of fociety, which the foolifh people are always looking up at, and ftaring, and diftracting themfelves with the integrity of its viciffitudes—to-day it is blown by the rough, rattling, tempeft of party; next day by the trade-wind of fly, fubtle, veering faction; then by the headlong hurricane of the people's hot foggy breath; huzza boys, down with the courtier, up with the patriot, 'till at laft the fmooth, foft, gentle warm breeze of intereft blows upon it, and from that moment it rufts to a point, and never ftirs after—fo there is your puff patriot for you—ogh, to the devil I pitch them all.

Counf. Ha, ha, ha! I am glad to find, brother, that you are come to that way of thinking at laft, and I wifh you had had the fame notions years ago, it would have faved you many thoufands.

O'Dogh. Indeed, and that it would—however, experience is an excellent tutor, and as you are a young man, and juft coming into the world, mine may be of fome fervice to you; take this judgment from me then, and remember that an honeft quiet country gentleman who out of policy and humanity eftablifhes manufactories, or that contrives employment for the idle and the induftrious, or that makes

but a blade of corn grow where there was none be-
fore, is of more ufe to this poor country than all the
courtiers, and patriots, and politicians, and prodi-
gals that are unhanged ;—fo there let us leave them,
and return to my wife's bufinefs.

Counf. With all my heart, I long to have a parti-
cular account of her conduct.

O'Dogh. O, brother, I have many grievances to
tell you of, but I have one that's more whimfical than
all the reft.

Counf. Pray what is it ?

O'Dogh. Why you muft know, brother, I am go-
ing to be a cuckold as faft as I can.

Counf. Ha, ha, ha ! that's a comical grievance in-
deed.

O'Dogh. O ftay till you hear the ftory, and I'll en-
gage you will fay it is as comical a cuckoldom as
ever was contrived.

Counf. I am glad to find, fir, it is of fo facetious
a nature—pray let me hear this bufinefs ?

O'Dogh. Sit down, then, brother, for I have got
a little touch of my gout, let us fit down for a mo-
ment, and I will let you into the whole affair.

Counf. Pray do, fir, for you have really raifed my
curiofity.   [*Sits.*]

O'Dogh. You muft know, brother, there is an
Englifh coxcomb in this town juft arrived among us,
who thinks every woman that fees him is in love with
him, and this fpark, like another Paris of Troy,
has taken it into his head to make a Helen of my
wife, and a poor cuckoldy Menelaus of me.

Counf. Ha, ha, ha! Pray who is the fpark?

O'Dogh. Why the name of this cuckold-maker
is Mufhroom, but from his conceit and impertinence,
the women and jokers of this town have dignified
him with the title of Count Mufhroom. Sir, he is
the fon of a pawn-broker in London, who having a
mind to make a gentleman of his fon, fent him to the
univerfity of Oxford; where, by mixing in the fol-
lies and vices of irregular youth, he got into a moft
fanguine friendfhip with young Lord Old-Caftle, who
you know has a large eftate in this country, and of
whofe anceftors mine have held long and profitable
leafes, which are now near expiring—in fhort, fir,
this fame Count Mufhroom and my lord became the
Pylades and Oreftes of the age, and fo very fond
was my lord of him, that out of fheer friendfhip to the
count, he got his fifter with child.

Counf. Ha, ha, ha! that was friendly indeed.

O'Dogh. O yes, it was what you may call modern
friendfhip, tafte, and *bon ton*; and my lord being a
man of gratitude, in return made him his agent in
this country, and fent him over to fettle his affairs
here. And the count and I being in treaty to renew
the leafes with my lord, and we not being able to
agree upon the terms, the coxcomb fends my wife a
warm billedoux, in which he very gallantly tells her
that fhe fhall decide the difference between us, and
fettle the leafes at her own price, only upon the tri-
fling condition that he may be permitted now and
then to be the occafional lord of her ladyfhip's matri-
monial manor.

Counf. Impudent rafcal! And, pray, what fays my fifter to all this?

O'Dogh. Why fhe does not know a word of the matter.

Counf. No! pray how came you to be acquainted with his letter then, and his defigns upon my fifter?

O'Dogh. Why there is the joke: it was by the help of Katty Farrel, my wife's woman, by whofe affiftance I carry on a correfpondence with the fellow in my wife's name, unknown to her; and by that means I fhall not only detect and expofe the fellow, but get an excellent bargain of the leafes, which are to be figned this very day.

Counf. But, fir, I hope you won't accept of leafes upon thofe terms.

O'Dogh. O, I have no time to moralize with you on that point, but depend upon it I will convince you before I fleep of the propriety of my taking the leafes: Lord, what figuifies it; it is only a good bargain got from a foolifh lord by the ingenuity of a knavifh agent, which is what happens every day in this country, and in every country indeed.

Enter JOHN.

John. Sir, Mr. Mufhroom and Mr. Sharp the attorney are below.

O'Dogh. O, they are come about the leafes. I will wait on them, John. [*Exit* John.]—Now, brother, you shall see one of the perfect and most conceited impudent coxcombs that has ever yet been imported into this land, or that disgraced humanity.

Mushroom [*without.*] My compliments, Mrs. Katty, to your lady, I will be with her in the twinkling of a star, or in less time than a single glance of her own immortal beauty can pass to the centre of an amorous heart.

O'Dogh. Orra now did you ever hear such cursed nonsense.

Enter MUSHROOM.

Mush. My dear Diggerty, I kiss your hands. I am come on purpose—I beg ten thousand pardons —I understood you were alone—you are busy I presume.

O'Dogh. Indeed, count, we are not. This gentleman is a relation—my wife's brother—Counsellor Hamilton, whom you have so often heard me talk of, and with whom I desire you will be acquainted.

Mush. Sir, I feel a superlative happiness in being known to you, I have long expected and long wished for it with a lover's appetite ; therefore without waiting for the dull avocation of experience, or the pedantic forms of ceremony, I beg you will honour me with a niche in your esteem, and register me in the select catalogue of your most constant and most ardent friends and admirers.

Counf. O dear fir, you are fuperabundantly obliging
—this is fuch a favour—

Mufh. No, no, no—none, none—give me your
hand, Hamilton, you are my friend Diggerty's
friend, and that's enough—I'll ferve you—fay no
more—I'll ferve you—rely upon me—I live in this
town quite *en famille*—I go about every where, am
of no party but thofe of love, pleafure and gallantry—
the women like and command me at cards, tea,
fcandal and dancing—the men, at wit, hazard, jolly
parties, a late hour and a bottle—I love eafe, hate
ceremony, and am at home wherever I go—that's
my fyftem, Hamilton—ha, is not that tafte, life,
philofophy, and *fummum bonum*—ha, my dear, at home
wherever l go, an't I, Diggerty?

O'Dogh. O, indeed, to give you your due, count,
you are never bafhful in any place.

Mufh. Never, never, my dear.

O'Dogh. No faith, nor none of your family I be-
lieve.

Mufh. Ha, ha, ha ! never, never, my dear Dig-
gerty—bafhfulnefs is a mark of ignorance, an un-
courtly, vulgar difeafe—what we men of the world
are never infected with—but, my dear Diggerty, I
am come on purpofe to fettle with you; my attorney
with the leafes is below, for as I know my lord
would be loth to lofe you as a tenant, and as I am
convinced it would be for his intereft you fhould have
the lands, why we will even fign and feal at once
upon your own terms—for really I think tenants in
Ireland want encouragement—they are rack'd too

high—they are indeed—it is a shame they should be rack'd so high.

O'Dogh. Faith, count, there's many a true word spoke in jest.

Mush. Upon my honour I am serious—you want encouragement in trade too.

O'Dogh. But do you really think so?

Mush. I do upon my honour, and I will speak to some people of consequence about it on the other side, as soon as I return.

O'Dogh. Orra but will you?

Mush. I will upon my honour.

O'Dogh. O aye, you politicians promise us the devil and all while you are among us, but the moment you get o't'other side, you have devilish bad memories.

Counf. You seem to like Ireland, sir.

Mush. O immensely, sir—it is a damn'd fine country, sir—and excellent claret—excellent claret upon my honour! 'tis true, indeed, it is not such claret as we drink in London—however, upon the whole, it's a pretty, neat, light, soft, silky, palateable wine, and I like it mightily—but your fish in this here country is horrid. There you want taste, Hamilton—that there is an article of the *savoir vivre*, in which you are totally ignorant—quite barbarous—

Counf. Aye! in what respect, sir?

Mush. Oh, my dear Hamilton, how can you ask such a question—you, you, now—who have been in London!—why you eat all your fish here too noo—

Counf. Too noo?

Mufh. Yes, all too noo—why you eat it the very day—nay, fometimes the very hour it comes out of the water—now that there is a total want of tafte—quite barbarous.

O'Dogh. O yes, brother, we eat all our fifh in this here country too noo—too noo a great deal. Now, I fancy, count, we fhould keep our fifh before we drefs it, as you keep your venifon, till it has got the hot gout.

Mufh. Ha, ha, ha!—the hot gout—ha, ha, ha! —Oh, I fhall expire—my dear Diggerty, I honour your hot gout—but your French is a little *en Irlandois—en Provence—haut gout* is the word.

O'Dogh. Yes, yes—I underftand you—Fogo.

Mufh. Ha, ha, ha!—Hamilton, you are a little odd in this here country in fome points—your friend there—is—you underftand me—however upon the whole, take you altogether, you are a damn'd honeft, tory rory, rantum fcantum, dancing, finging, laughing, boozing, jolly, friendly, fighting, hofpitable people, and I like you mightily.

Omnes. Ha, ha, ha!

Counf. Upon my word, fir, the people of Ireland are much obliged to you for your helter fkelter, rantum fcantum portrait of them.

O'Dogh. Indeed and that we are; and fo you like us mightily?

Mufh. I do upon honour, and I believe I fhall marry one of your women here, grow domeftic, and fettle among you.

O'Dogh. Orra but will you do us that honour?

Mush. I really intend it.

O'Dogh. Faith then you will be a great honour to us, and you will find a great many relations here, count; for we have a large crop of the Mushrooms in this here country.

Mush. O, sir, I don't doubt it, for we are a numerous family both in England and Ireland—but I beg pardon, my dear Diggerty, I must rob you of my company for a moment to pay my devoirs to your lady; I know she is impatient to see me upon a particular affair—I will return upon the wings of diligence, then sign, squeeze wax, and dedicate to wit, mirth, and convivial jollity—Hamilton, yours, yours—my dear Diggerty, give me thy hand—from this moment set me down as thy unalterable friend—for I intend to be well with thy wife this very evening. 　　　　　　　　　　　　　　　　[*Exit.*

O'Dogh. Sure there never was so conceited and so impertinent a coxcomb as this puppy.

Enter KATTY FARREL.

Oh here is Katty Farrel. So, Katty, do you see who's here, child—your friend the counsellor.

Katty. Sir, your humble servant, I am glad to see you look so well. I hope all your good family are in health.

Counf. All very well, I thank you, Mrs. Katty.

O'Dogh. Well, well, now your ceremonies are

over, let us to bufinefs—is your fine miftrefs dreffed
yet?

Katty. Yes, fir—but fhe has had a fad misfortune.

O'Dogh. What is that, Katty?

Katty. The money, fir, that you gave her to pay
the mercer's bill, from Covent-Garden, that was
fent after her, fhe loft laft night to my Lady Kin-
negad, and fome more of them, at bragg—but do
not take any notice that I have told you of it, for fhe
intends to borrow as much from Mr. Mufhroom for
a day or two as will pay the bill.

Counf. Why the woman has loft all fenfe of fhame.
—[*Afide.*]

O'Dogh. Katty, that muft not be. She muft not
do fo mean a thing upon any account, as to borrow
money of Mufhroom. I will let you have the mo-
ney to pay the bill, and do you fay you borrowed it
of your brother, or fome friend or other, for her.

Katty. I will, fir.   [*Exit.*

[*Mrs.* Diggerty, Mufhroom, *&c.* laugh *very*
    loud *without.*]

O'Dogh. So, the toilet council is broke up at laft
—here fhe comes, as fantaftically fine, as a fine lady
in a play. Ogho, what a head fhe has.

Enter Mrs. DIGGERTY *and* MUSHROOM.

Mrs. Dig. Brother, I am veeftly glad to fee
you.

Counf. Welcome from England, fifter.

Mrs. Dig. I am imminſely obligated to you, brother.

Counſ. I hope it anſwered your expectation, ſiſter.

Mrs. Dig. Tranſcendantly.

Counſ. I am glad it pleaſed you.

Mrs. Dig. Raviſhingly.

Counſ. Indeed!

Mrs. Dig. Beyond all degrees of compiriſon.

O'Dogh. O yes—beyond all degrees of compiriſon.

Mrs. Dig. Veeſt! imminſe! extatic! I never knew life before—every thing there is high, tip top, the grand monde, the bun tun—and quite teeſty.

O'Dogh. O yes, every thing there is quite teeſty, brother.

Mrs. Dig. Well, count, do you know that you pleaſed me veeſtly laſt night; I never ſaw you in ſuch high humour—brother, I believe you do not know Mr. Muſhroom, an Engliſh gentleman; pray let me have the honour of introducing him to you.

Counſ. I have had that honour already, ſiſter.

Muſh. Yes, madam, Hamilton and I are old acquaintance.

O'Dogh. O yes they are old acquaintance, they have known each other above theſe two minutes.

Counſ. Pray how do you like London, ſiſter?

Mrs. Dig. O the place of the world, brother.

Counſ. Then Dublin I ſuppoſe—

Mrs. Dig. O, dear brother, don't neem them together.

O'Dogh. O no, you muſt not neem them toge-
ther.

Mrs. Dig. Upon my honour, Dublin, after ſeeing
London, looks like Iriſh-town or Ring's-end : Oh,
every thing I ſet my eyes on here gives me the *ennui*,
and the *countre cure.*

O'Dogh. O yes, every thing here gives her the
contre cœur ; that is a diſeaſe ſhe has brought over
with her from London that we know nothing of
here.

Mrs. Dig. The ſtreets are ſo narrow, the houſes
ſo dirty, and the people ſo ridiculous ! then the wo-
men, count ! ha, ha, ha !—I can't help laughing
when I think of them. Well, I am convinced that
the women of this here country who have never tra-
velled, have nothing of that—a—a—non chalance,
and that jenny-ſee-quee that we have in London.

O'Dogh. O no, brother ! the women have nothing
of that jenny-ſee-quee, that ſhe has brought over with
her from London.

Mrs. Dig. But, Muſhroom—I don't know if what
I am going to tell you be conceit or real ; but, upon
my honour, when I firſt came from England—you
muſt know, brother, I came over in the picket.

O'Dogh. O yes, brother, ſhe came over in the
picket.

Mrs. Dig. Yes, ſir, I came over in the picket, and
we had a great orage —I don't believe, Mr. Diggerty,
you know what an orage is.

O'Dogh. Indeed you may take your oath I don't,
my dear.

Mrs. Dig. That is, fir, becafe you have not been in foreign parts—then I will tell you what an orage is—fir, an orage is a ftorum.

O'Dogh. Madam, I thank you for your intelligence—indeed you are very learned and very obliging.

Mrs. Dig. And fo, as I was faying, count, we had a great ftorum, and the picket—I fhall never forget it—the picket landed us about twenty miles from Dublin—and fo, do you know, I fay, Mufhroom, that I fancied, being juft come from England, that the very dogs here when they barked, had the brogue, ha, ha, ha!

Omnes. Ha, ha, ha!

Mufh. Why then, by all that's gothic, madam, I have thought fo a thoufand times.

Mrs. Dig. You have!

Mufh. I have, upon honour.

Mrs. Dig. Have you ever obferved it, brother? Mr. Diggerty, what do you think? Hav'n't the dogs of this here country the brogue?

O'Dogh. Indeed and that they have, my dear, and the cows too, and the fheep, and the bullocks, and that as ftrong as ever your own mother had it, who was an O'Gallagher.

Mrs. Dig. Oh!

O'Dogh. Not two of whofe anceftors could ever fpeak three words of Englifh to be underftood.

Mrs. Dig. You are a ftrange rude man, Mr. Diggerty, to tell me of my mother's family—you know I always defpifed my mother's family—I hate the

very name of Gallagher, and all the old Irish what-
ever.

Counf. The prefent company excepted, fifter—
your hufband, you know—

Mrs. Dig. O, I never think of him.

Counf. Ha, that's polite indeed.

O'Dogh. O no, fhe never thinks of me.

Counf. Well, but fifter, you have given us no ac-
count of the coronation, no doubt you were there.

Mrs. Dig. There! O moundew!—What a quif-
tion! Why I was in every part of it—ax Mufhroom
elfe.

Mufh. Every where, every where—fhe was every
where, and with every body.

O'Dogh. Well, well—then I fuppofe it was very
fine; but after all now, was it as fine as our riding
the fringes here, or the lord lieutenant going to the
parliament houfe.

Mrs. Dig. He, he, he! O fhocking! don't neem
them together—now that is fo Irifh—but, brother,
what would have afforded you the higheft entertain-
ment, was the city feaft. O that there was im-
minfe.

O'Dogh. O yes, that there was imminfe, brother,
and much finer than this here.

Counf. Then you were at the city feaft too, fif-
ter?

Mrs. Dig. O dear, yes! the court never ftirred
without me.

O'Dogh. No, indeed, the court never ftirred with-
out her.

Mrs. Dig. And the lord mayor made a point of having me there : so I went with her grace, a friend of mine, and a party of the court, as one of the houshold—but the minute I went in every eye was upon me : Lord, it was veestly pleasant to see how the she grocers, the she mercers, the she dyers, the she hosiers, and the she taylors did stare at me—I was very brilliant that's certain—rather more so than I was at the wedding.

O'Dogh. O indeed I don't doubt but you were a sight.

Mrs. Dig. O pray, Mr. Diggerty, be quiet, and don't interrupt me.—Well, but, brother, as I was saying, it was imminsely entertaining to hear the awkward city creatures whisper and give their vardee upon me, in their city manner— Lord, is this the handsome Irishwoman ?—the famous Irish toast ?—the celebrated Mrs. Diggerty—ha !—I don't think she is so handsome, says one—hum !—well enough, says another, only I don't like her nose—pray, doesn't she squint ? says a third—O yes, she certainly squints, says a fourth—and she is a little crooked —but she is genteel—O yes, yes, the city creatures all allowed I was genteel.

O'Dogh. O yes, yes, to be sure they all allowed she was genteel.

Mrs. Dig. But, brother—O Lud ! I had like to have forgot—do you know that the count is one of the prettiest poets in England, aye, or in Ireland either.

Musb. O heavens ! madam !

Mrs. Dig. He is, by my honour.

Counf. I do not doubt the gentleman's talents in the leaft, fifter.

Mufh. Sir, you are very polite, the lady is pleas'd to rally, that's all, for my mufe is but a fmatterer—a flattern—a mere flip-fhod lady.

Mrs. Dig. Do not mind him, brother, what I fay is true. He is a mighty pretty poet, and to convince you that he is, I will fhew you fome verfes that he indited upon me, as I was dancing at court—[*Pulls them out.*]—Here they are, brother: Count, will you be fo obliging as to read them to my brother ?

Mufh. Madam, as the fublime bard politely fings, the nod of beauty fways both gods and men, and I obey. Gentlemen, the title will at once let you into the whole of what you are to expect in this little production. *An extempore on the famous Mrs. O' Diggerty's dancing at court.*—Now attend—

> *When beauteous Diggerty leads up the dance*
> *In fair Britannia's court,*
> *Then ev'ry heart is in a prance,*
> *And longs for Cupid's fport.*
> *Beaux ogle, and pant and gaze,*
> *Belles envy and fneer, yet praife,*
> *As Venus herfelf were there ;*
> *And prudes agree, it muft be fhe,*
> *It muft be fhe—or Diggerty,*
> *It muft be fhe—or Diggerty,*
> *Or Diggerty, the fair.*

[*Bows very low to Mrs.* Diggerty.
That's all, gentlemen, that's all—only a *jeu d'efprit,*

as I told you; a slight effort of a muse, bound in
the silken chains of beauty and delight.

[*He bows, she curtseys.*

Counf. Conceited coxcomb ! [*Aside.*]

Mush. And now, madam, I have a favour to beg
of you.

Mrs. Dig. O command it—what is it ?

Mush. Why, madam, as the celebrated Doctor
Thomas Augustus Arne has honoured this hasty
offspring with an alliance of his harmonious muse,
and as your ladyship has frequently heretofore enli-
vened it with your vocal glee, shall we beg that you
will once more animate these verbal images with a
touch of your Promethean pipe.

Mrs. Dig. O dear, count, you are veestly panegy-
rical.

Counf. Aye, aye, come, sister, as you have the tune
oblige us with it.

Mrs. Dig. I will try, brother, what I can do—
but, by my honour, I have a great big cold—hem,
hem !—

Mush. The worse your voice, madam, the more
your taste will shine.

Mrs. Dig Nay, count, voice or no voice, I will
make an effort—Sol-la-mi-fa-sol, &c.—Upon my ho-
nour I have no more voice than a kitling.

S O N G.

[*During the song* Mushroom *beats time conceitedly,
but so as not to interrupt her, or interfere with her
acting it.*]

Mu/b. Bravo! braviffimo! cariffimo! novelliffimo! tranfcendiffimo! and every fuperlativiffimo in the fublime region of excellentiffimo!

O' Dogh. Come, count, now if you pleafe we will go down, and fign the leafes, and difpatch the attornies.

Mu/b. With all my heart.   [*Exit* O'Dogh.

Mrs. Dig. You dine here, count.

Mu/b. Do I breathe! do I exift! I will but juft ftep down, fign the leafes, and return on the wings of inclination—*ma chere belle fans,* adieu.   [*Exit.*

Mrs. Dig. Au revoir—well, he is a moft humourous creature, and mighty witty : don't you think fo, brother?

Counf. Very witty, indeed, and I fuppofe underftands a lady's toilet—

Mrs. Dig. The beft of any man in the world, the moft handy creature about a woman—and fuch teeft—but, brother, you muft fup with us to-night— I have a few friends—a private peerty this evening : Lady Kinnegad, Lady Pam, old Lady Bab Frightful, Mrs. Gazette, Mr. Mufhroom, Pat Fitzmungrel, Major Gamble, Mrs. Cardmark, and half a fcore more—quite a private peerty—you muft be with us, brother—we are to have a little gambling and dancing, and are to be mighty jolly—I fhall expeft you—yours, yours—I muft go finifh my toilet.

[*Exit.*

Counf. What a ftrange turn this woman's mind has taken—fhe is far gone I fee, and muft be pinched to the quick—and fhall this very night.   [*Exit.*

ACT II. SCENE I.

Enter Mr. and Mrs. O'DOGHERTY.

O'Dogherty.

WELL, but, my dear, why will you be in such a paffion ? Why will you not hearken to reafon ?

Mrs. Dig. Mr. Diggerty, I will hear no reafon ; there can be no reafon againft what I fay—you are the ftrangeft man—not be a lord—fir, I infift upon it —there's a neceffity for a peerage.

O'Dogh. O ! then only fhew me the neceffity, and all my objections will vanifh.

Mrs. Dig. Why, fir, I am affronted for want of a title : a parcel of upftarts, with their crownets upon their coaches, their chairs, their fpoons, their handkerchiefs—nay, on the very knockers of their doors —creatures that were below me but t'other day, are now truly my fuperiors, and have the precedency, and are fet above me at table.

O'Dogh. Set above you at table ?

Mrs. Dig. Yes, fir, fet above me at table wherever I go.

O'Dogh. Upon my honour then that's a great fhame.

·G

Well, well, my dear—come, come, my dear, don't be in such a fluster.

Mrs. Dig. Fluster! why sir, I tell you I am ready to expire whenever I go into the great world.

O'Dogh. At what, my dear ?

Mrs. Dig. At what—Egh! how can you ax such an ignorant quistion? Can there be any thing more provoking to a woman of my teest and spirit, than to hear the titles of a parcel of upstart ugly creatures bawled in one's ears upon every occasion—my Lady Kinnegad's coach there—my Lady Kilgobbin's chair there—my Lady Castleknock's servants there—my Lady Tanderagee's chariot there. And after all these titles only consider how my vile neem sounds. [*Cries.*] Mrs. Diggerty's servants there—Mrs. Diggerty's chair there—Mrs. Diggerty's coach there —it is so mean and beggarly I cannot bear it—the very thought of it makes me ready to burst my stays, and almost throws me into my hysterics. [*Throws herself into a couch.*

O'Dogh. Nay, my dear, don't be working yourself up to your fits, your hysterics, and your tantrums now.

Mrs. Dig. My life is miserable. [*Rises.*] You cross me in every thing, you are always finding fault with my routs, and my drums, and my fancy ball— t'other night you would not make up a dress for it, nor appear at it—O fie, fie, fie—but you are true Irish to the very bone of you.

O'Dogh. Indeed I am, and to the marrow within the bone too ; and what is more, I hope I shall never be otherwise.

Mrs. Dig. Ridiculous weaknefs! Pray, fir, do not you think the Englifh love their country as well as the Irifh do theirs?

O'Dogb. O indeed I believe they do, and a great deal better; though we have a great many among us that call themfelves patriots and champions, who, at the fame time, would not care if poor old Ireland was fqueezed as you fqueeze an orange—provided they had but their fhare of the juice.

Mrs. Dig. Pooh, pooh! nobody minds what you fay—you are always abufing every body in power— well, fir, you fee the Englifh are improving in teeft every day, and have their burlettas and their operas, their Cornelys, their Almacks, their macaronies—

O'Dogb. O my dear, I tell you again and again, that the Englifh can never be precedent to us. They, by their genius and conftitution, muft always run mad about fomething or other, either about burlettas, pantomimes, a man in a bottle, a Cock-lane ghoft, or fomething of equal importance. But, my dear, they can afford to run mad after fuch nonfenfe; why they owe more money than we are worth; ftay 'till we are as rich as they are, and then we may be allowed to run mad after abfurdities as well as they.

Mrs. Dig. Mighty well, fir, mighty well! Oh mighty well.

O'Dogb. Heyday, what's the matter now?

Mrs. Dig. But I fee your defign—you have a mind to break my heart—[*Sobs and cries.*]—yes, you argue and contradict me for no other end—you do every thing to fret and vex me.

O'Dogh. Pray explain, my dear? What is it you mean?

Mrs. Dig. Why, fir, ever fince I returned to this odious country I have been requefting and begging, and praying, that you would fend to London only for the fet of long-tailed horfes, that I told you I admired fo—but no, I cannot prevail, though you know my Lady Kilgobbin, my Lady Balruddery, my Lady Caftleknock, and, in fhort, every lady of figure all run upon long tails—nobody but doctors, apothecaries, lawyers, cits, and country fquires drive with fhort tails now—for my part, you know I deteft a fhort tail.

O'Dogh. Well, my dear, I have fent for your brother to town, on purpofe to fettle all thefe points between us, and if he thinks it proper that you fhould have long tails, you may have them as long as my Lady Kilgobbin's, my Lady Balruddery's tails, or any tails in the univerfe ; and as to the title, if it can be had, why we will fubmit that to him likewife.

Mrs. Dig. I know it can be had—and fo let me have no more trouble about it, for a title I will have —I muft be a lady as well as other people—I can't bear being a plain Mrs. Diggerty any longer.— [*Cries.*]

O'Dogh. Well, well, my dear, we will try what we can do—you muft be a lady ! yes, yes, you fhall be a lady ; but by the blood of the O'Dogherty's, it fhall be a broken-back'd lady. A hump fhall be your patent, my dear. [*Afide.*]   [*Exit.*

Mrs. Dig. An obstinate man ! not accept of a title —in short, there's no living without it. Who's there ?

Enter JOHN.

John. Madam !

Mrs. Dig. Nobody come yet ?

John. No, madam.

Mrs. Dig. What's o'clock ?

John. A quarter past seven, madam.

Mrs. Dig. Are the candles lit, and the cards ready ?

John. They have been ready this half hour, madam.

Mrs. Dig. Shew the company into this room.

John. Yes, madam.

[*A loud knocking, three servants without.*]

Will. Lady Kinnegad.

James. Lady Kinnegad.

John. Lady Kinnegad.

Enter JOHN, *shewing in Lady* KINNEGAD.

John. Lady Kinnegad, madam.   [*Exit.*

L. Kin. My dear Diggy—what, all alone—nobody come ?

Mrs. Dig. Not a mortal, I have been fretting this this hour at being alone, and had nothing to divert me but a quarrel with my husband.

L. Kin. The old fogrum! what, he won't open his purfe ftrings, I fuppofe—but you fhould make him, for he is as rich as a Jew.

Mrs Dig. Aye, but he is as clofe-fifted as an old judge—Lord, he has no notion of any thing in life, but reading mufty books, draining bogs, planting trees, eftablifhing manufactories, fetting the common people to work, and faving money.

L. Kin. Ha, ha, ha! the monfter!

[*A loud knocking.*

Will. Major Gamble.
James. Major Gamble.
John. Major Gamble.

Enter JOHN *and Major* GAMBLE.

John. Major Gamble, madam.   [*Exit.*

Mrs. Dig. Major, how is your gout to-day?

Major. I don't know how the devil it is, not I—hobbling up your ftairs has made me fweat— Lady Kinnegad, I kifs your hands; I afk your pardon, but I muft fit down—I cannot ftand—I got cold laft night, and I feel it to-day—what, is there nobody come yet but us—nothing going forward.

[*Loud knocking.*

Will. Lady Bab Frightful.
James. Lady Bab Frightful.
John. Lady Bab Frightful.

L. Kin. Here fhe comes, as Mufhroom fays, nature's contradiction—youth and age, froft and fire, winter and fummer, an old body and a young mind.

Enter John *and Lady* Bab Frightful.

John. Lady Bab Frightful, Madam.   [*Exit.*
Mrs. Dig. My dear Lady Bab!
L. Bab. My dear Diggy—Lady Kinnegad, I kiſs
your hands—O, major—why you had like to have
ruined us all laſt night—the bank was juſt broke—
well, I am a perfect rake—I think I was one of the
laſt this morning. I danced till five.
L. Kin. As the old ſaying is, Lady Bab—you can
never do it younger—Live while we live, that's the
rule of happineſs, you have good ſpirits, a good join-
ture, and nobody to controul you—you amiable crea-
ture.
L. Bab. Yes, I thank my ſtars, I never want
ſpirits, tol, lol, lol, [*ſings*]—I could dance till morn-
ing.
                              [*Loud knocking.*
Will. Mrs. Jolly.
James. Mrs. Jolly.
John. Mrs. Jolly.

Enter John *and Mrs.* Jolly.

John. Mrs. Jolly, madam.
                [*Gives a card to Mrs.* Dig. *and exit.*
Mrs. Jolly. So, good folks.
Mrs. Dig. Madam, your moſt obedient.
Mrs. Jolly. What, all idle!—no loo—no brag—

no hazard—nor no dancing begun yet, and Lady
Bab here—but where's Mushroom—I've such a story
for him.—Where's the Count Diggerty?

Enter JOHN *with a note and exit.*

Mrs. Dig. O he will be here, never fear, madam
—O-this is a card from Gazette. [*reads*] *Dear Dig,
I cannot be with you at seven; but before you have play'd
two hands, expect me—three short visits at the Green,
one in Merrion-street, two in the Mall, in Britain-street,
three words at the Castle with his Excellency, and then I
am yours for the night, and whilst I am——Gazette.*

L. Kin. Well said, Gazette!—she will spread
more scandal in these short visits than truth can re-
move in a twelvemonth.

[*Loud knocking.*

Will. Mr. Fitzmungrel.

James. Mr. Fitzmungrel.

John. Mr. Fitzmungrel.

L. Kin. O, here's Fitzmungrel! drunk, I suppose,
according to custom.

L. Bab. And brutal, according to nature; yes,
yes, he's drunk I see. I will be gone, for I know he
will be rude.

L. Kin. No, no, stay—let us all share in his abuse,
pray.

Enter JOHN.

John. Mr. Fitzmungrel, madam. [*Exit.*

Enter FITZMUNGREL, *drunk and finging.*

Fitz. My dear, Mrs. O'Dogherty—but I know you do not love to be called O'Dogherty, and therefore I will call you by your Englifh name, Mrs. Diggerty—my dear Diggerty, I have not been in bed fince I faw you.

Mrs. Dig. Why where have you been, Fitz ?

Fitz. At the Curragh, my dear, with Pat. Wildfire, Sir Anthony All-Night, Sir Toby Ruin, Dick Bafhaw, and half a fcore more, and a fine chafe we had—haux, haux, my honies—over, over, haux—but I was refolved to be with you, my little Diggerty, becaufe I promifed, fo I fmoaked it away to town—drove myfelf in my own Phaeton, and was over-turned juft as I came to dirty Dublin.

Mrs. Dig. Why you are all dirty ?

Fitz. Yes, I had a fine fet down in the dirtieft fpot of the whole road.

Mrs. Dig. I hope you are not hurt ?

Fitz. Not I, my dear—haux—haux—whoop—no, no, my dear Diggerty, I am like a cat—I always light upon my legs—haux—haux—whoop—ha, my dear angelic coufin, Lady Bab Frightful—by heavens, you are a beautiful creature, and look like the picture of good luck—well, fhall we have another bank to night ?—here, take this note into your bank [*gives a note*] I will go take a nap in the next room in my old chair, and when you have made it five hundred, wake me, my little babby—do you hear—

L. Bab. I will, I will—that's a good man, go, and
take a nap.

Fitz. My dear coufin, thou'rt the beauty of our
family.

L. Bab. Well, well—go fleep—go fleep.

Fitz. The beauty of our family, Bab—another Ve-
nus—as handfome as Medufa, and you are befides a
good-natured, old, young, middle-aged, giggling girl
of three-fcore—fo I'll go take my nap—haux—haux
—tally ho—whoop—   [*Exit.*

Mrs. Dig. He is horrid drunk.

L. Kin. And what is worfe, he is a greater brute
fober than drunk.

[*Loud knocking.*

Will. Mrs. Gazette.

James. Mrs. Gazette.

John. Mrs. Gazette.

L. Kin. Here fhe comes, that knows every body's
bufinefs but her own, ha, ha, ha !

Major. I will fwear fhe is in as many houfes every
day as Faulkner's Journal.

Enter John *and Mrs.* Gazette.

John. Mrs. Gazette, madam.   [*Exit.*

Mrs. Gaz. My dear Diggerty, you got my billet—
I came to you as foon as poffible—but where's Mufh-
room—I do not fee him.

Mrs. Dig. He will be here, madam.

Mrs. Gaz. My dear Jolly, why you look in high
bloom to-night—Major, how's your gout—Lady Kin-

.negad, your moſt devoted—Oh, but Diggerty, I have a piece of news--they ſay your huſband's to have a peerage.

Omnes. Ha, ha, ha !

Mrs. Dig. It is very true, madam, very true—we are to be entitled.

Mrs. Gaz. Why not ? I am ſure there are thoſe, that have not half your fortune, who have got peerages. And pray, my dear, what is your title to be —you muſt conſult me upon it.

Mrs. Dig. Why, I have thought of ſeveral, but know not which to pitch upon—I am diſtracted. about it, I have thought of nothing elſe this week— I wiſh you would all adviſe me—it muſt be ſomething new, elegant, and uncommon—and teeſty—yes, I muſt have it teeſty---ſee, here is the liſt of titles--if you will all ſtep into the drawing-room, we will determine upon one, and then ſit down to our peerties —come, *alons---ſans ceremonie---*I'll ſhew you the way —come, major——   [*Exeunt all but the* Major.

Major. Aye, aye, pack along---I'll hobble after you. —get the hazard ready—but I muſt ſit by the fire--- I am curſed lame—'ſblood, I have trod upon ſome damn'd ſhell or pebble—O damn it --curſe the ſhell --but Lady Bab's bank will be worth touching.

[*Exit.*

Enter O'Dogherty *and Katty* Farrel.

O'Dogh. They are all gone to their nightly devotions---well, and what did ſhe ſay when you gave her the money ?

Katty. O fir, fhe was overjoy'd, and fo thankful
—but fhe will lofe it all again to that Lady Kinne-
gad.

O'Dogh. Not to-night, Katty; her brother was in
the room before them to prevent her playing; he is
refolved to fettle all affairs with her this very night.
But what makes this Mufhroom ftay fo long? Sure
he will come.

Katty. O never fear, fir—you never faw a man fo
eager, and fo full of expectation.

O'Dogh And fo you have really dreffed him up in
your lady's clothes?

Katty. I have, fir, indeed—and he is ten times fon-
der of himfelf (if poffible) as a woman, I think, than
he was as a man.

O'Dogh. Ogh I will engage I will cure him of his
paffion for himfelf, and for all Irifh women, as long
as he lives.

Katty. Here comes my miftrefs, and her brother
with her, fir.

O'Dogh. Come, come, quick; let us get out of their
way, for he is refolved to ftartle the lady, and waken
her, if poffible. Let us leave them to themfelves,
for I reckon they will have a fharp brufh.

[*Exeunt.*

Enter Mrs. DIGGERTY *and* HAMILTON.

Coun. Madam, madam, you fhall hear me.

Mrs. Dig. Was there ever fo rude, fo abrupt a be-
haviour—to force me from my company thus.

Coun. 'Tis what your infolent difeafe demands; the fuddennefs and abruptnefs of the fhock is the chief ingredient in the remedy that muft cure you.

Mrs. Dig. What do you mean, fir?

Coun. I will tell you, madam—you are not igno-rant that your hufband took you without a fortune; that he generoufly gave the little our father left you to your younger fifter, with the benevolent addition of two thoufand pounds—you know too, that by marriage articles, upon a feparation or your hufband's death, you are entitled only to a hundred pounds a year; which cautious pittance his prudence wifely infifted on, as a neceffary check upon the conduct of giddy, female youth, and thoughtlefs vanity, when matched with the tempered age of fobriety and difcretion—now, madam, I am commiffioned to in-form you, that the doors are open, and that the fti-pulated fum will be punctually paid you, as your vi-cious appetite fhall demand; for know, that neither your hufband's love, my affection, nor a refidence in this houfe can be enjoyed by you another hour, but on the hard condition of a thorough reformation.

Mrs. Dig. Sir!

Coun. Madam, it is true; for if female vanity will be mad, hufbands muft be peremptory.

Mrs. Dig. Pray, fir, do not fpeak fo loud.

Coun. Why not?

Mrs. Dig. The company will hear you.

Coun. I know it—and I intend they fhall.

Mrs. Dig. Oh, oh, oh! I fhall be afhamed for ever—pray do not fpeak fo loud—blefs me, brother, you ftartle me—what is it you mean?

Coun. Will you hear what I have to fay ? Will you attend to the dictates of a brother's love, with modest patience, and virtuous candour ?

Mrs. Dig. I will.

Coun. Sit down—know then, in your husband's judgment, the fums you have fquandered, and thofe you have been cheated of by your female friends, is your leaft offence—it is your pride, your midnight revels, infolence of tafte, rage of precedency, that grieve him ; for they have made you the ridicule of every flirt and coxcomb, and the fcorn and pity of every fober perfon that knows your folly; this reflects difgrace upon your friends, contempt upon the fpirit and credit of your husband, and has furnifhed whifpering fufpicion with ftories and implications, which have fecretly fixed an infectious ftain upon your chaftity.   [*Both rife.*]

Mrs. Dig. My chaftity ! I defy the world !

Coun. Aye, madam, you may defy it; but fhe who does, will find the world too hard a match for her.

Mrs. Dig. I care not what flander fays—I will rely upon my innocence.

Coun. But I will not, madam, nor fhall you—it is not fufficient for my fifter, your husband's wife, or female reputation, to rely on innocence alone— women muft not only be innocent, they muft appear fo too.

Mrs. Dig. Brother, I don't know what you mean by all this. I beg you will explain.

Coun. I will—know then, this coxcomb Mufhroom——

Mrs. Dig. Mufhroom !

Coun. Mufhroom !—as a man of wit and fpirit, thought himfelf obliged to take fome hints your levity had given him.

Mrs. Dig. I give him hints—brother, you wrong me.

Coun. Pray hear me—this fpark, I fay, like a true man of intrigue, not only returns your hints with a letter of gallantry, but bribes your own woman to deliver it.

Mrs. Dig. My woman !

Coun. The fame.

Mrs. Dig. I am ignorant of all this, and will turn her out of the houfe this inftant.

Coun. Softly ! hear the whole ! the maid, inftead of carrying the letter to you, delivers that, and many others, to her mafter, who, in your name, hand, ftile, and fentiment, has anfwered them all, and carried on an amorous correfpondence with the gentleman, even up to an affignation ; and, now, at this very inftant, the fpark is preparing for the happy interview, and has made the town the confidants of his good fortune.

Mrs. Dig. O heavens !

Coun. Now judge what your hufband, brother, and your friends muft feel, and what the world muft think of her, whofe conduct could entitle a coxcomb to fuch liberties.

Mrs. Dig. Brother, I fhall make no defence—the ftory fhocks me ! and though I know my own intentions, yet what people may fay—but, be affured, I shall be more prudent for the future—perhaps I have been to blame—pray advise me—only say what I shall do to be revenged upon the fellow for his impudence, and what will convince my husband, you, and all the world of my innocence, and I will do it. I protest you have given such a motion to my heart, and such a trouble and a trembling, as it never felt before.

Coun. It is a virtuous motion—encourage it—for the anxiety and tears of repentance, though the rarest, are the brightest ornaments a modern fine lady can be deck'd in.

KATTY *and* O'DOGHERTY *without.*

O'Dogh. I shall be in here with the counsellor, Katty, and the moment he comes, bring me word.

Katty. I shall, sir.

Coun. Here your husband comes.

Mrs. Dig. I am ashamed to see him.

Enter O'DOGHERTY.

O'Dogh. Well, brother, have you spoke to her?

Coun. There she is, sir—and as she should be—bathed in the tears of humility and repentance.

O'Dogh Ogh! I am sorry to see this indeed—I am afraid you have gone too far. If I had been by, I assure you, brother, you should not have made her cry.—Yerrow, Nancy, child, turn about, and don't be crying there.

Mrs. Dig. Sir, I am ashamed to see your face—my errors I acknowledge—and for the future---

O'Dogh. Pooh, pooh—I will have no submissions nor acknowledgments ; if you have settled every thing with your brother, that is sufficient.

Mrs. Dig. I hope he is satisfied—and it shall be the business of my life---

O'Dogh. Pooh, pooh ! say no more I tell you, but come, give me a kiss, and let us be friends at once---there.--so, in that kiss, now, let all tears and uneasiness subside with you, as all fears and resentment shall-die with me.

Coun. Come, sister, give me your hand, for I must have my kiss of peace too.   I own I have been a little severe with you, but your disease required sharp medicines.

O'Dogh. Now we are friends, Nancy, I have a favour or two to beg of you.

Mrs. Dig. Pray, command them.

O'Dogh. Why, then, the first thing that I ask, is, that you will send away that French rascal the cook, with his compots and combobs, his alamodes and aladobes, his crapandoes and frigandoes, and a thousand outlandish kickshaws, that I am sure were never designed for Christian food ; and let the good rough rumps of beef, the jolly surloins, the geese and turkies, cram fowls, bacon and greens ; and the pies, puddings and pasties, that used to be perfectly shoving one another off of the table, so that there was not room for the people's plates ; with a fine large cod too, as big as a young alderman---I say, let all those

French kickſhaws be baniſhèd from my table, and theſe good old Iriſh diſhes be put in their places; and then the poor every day will have ſomething to eat.

Mrs. Dig. They ſhall, ſir.

O'Dogh. And as to yourſelf, my dear Nancy, I hope I ſhall never have any more of your London Engliſh; none of your this here's, your that there's, your winegars, your weals, your vindors, your toaſt-eſſes, and your ſtone poſteſſes; but let me have our own good plain, old Iriſh Engliſh, which I inſiſt upon is better than all the Engliſh Engliſh that ever coquets and coxcombs brought into the land.

Mrs. Dig. I will get rid of theſe as faſt as poſſible.

O'Dogh. And pray, above all things, never call me Mr. Diggerty—my name is Murrogh O'Dogherty, and I am not aſhamed of it; but that damn'd name Diggerty always vexes me whenever I hear it.

Mrs. Dig. Then, upon my honour, Mr. O'Dogherty, it ſhall never vix you again.

O'Dogh. Ogh, that's right, Nancy—O'Dogherty for ever—O'Dogherty!—there's a ſound for you—why they have not ſuch a name in all England as O'Dogherty—nor as any of our fine ſounding Mileſian names—what are your Jones and your Stones, your Rice and your Price, your Heads and your Foots, and Hands, and your Wills, and Hills and Mills, and Sands, and a parcel of little pimping names that a man would not pick out of the ſtreet, compared to the O'Donovans, O'Callaghans, O'Sullivans, O'Bral-laghans, O'Shaghneſſes, O'Flahertys, O'Gallaghers,

and O'Doghertys,---Ogh, they have courage in the
very found of them, for they come out of the mouth
like a ftorm ; and are as old and as ftout as the oak
at the bottom of the bog of Allen, which was there
before the flood---and though they have been difpof-
feffed by upftarts and foreigners, buddoughs and faf-
fanoughs, yet I hope they will flourish in the Ifland of
Saints, while grafs grows or water runs.

Enter Katty.

Katty. Mr. Mufhroom is come, fir.

O'Dogh. What, in his woman's cloaths ?

Katty. Yes, fir.

O'Dogh. Impudent rafcal ! and where have you put
him, Katty?

Katty. In the back parlour, fir.

O'Dogh. Odzooks ! Katty, go down, and fhew
him up here---this is the largeft room to exercife the
gentleman in---begone, quick, and leave all the reft to
me.

Katty. I am gone, fir.   [*Exit.*

O'Dogh. My dear, you muft act a part in this farce ;
the better to bring the rafcal into ridicule.

Mrs. Dig. Any thing to be revenged of him for his
ill opinion of me.

O'Dogh. Step into your own room, then, and I
will come and inftruct you how to behave.   And
                              [*Exit Mrs.* Dig.
brother, do you go and open the affair to the com-

pany, and bring them here to liften to the Count's gallantry, and to be witneffes of his making me a cuckold.

Coun. I warrant you I will prepare them for the fcene. But, brother, be fure you make the gentleman fmart.   [*Exit.*

O'Dogh. Cgh, leave him to me—by the honour of the whole Irifh nation I will make him remember the name of Diggerty, as fenfibly as ever his fchool-mafter did hic, hæc, hoc, genitivo hujus—an impudent raf- cal! make a cuckold of an Irifhman—what, take our own trade out of our hands—and a branch of bufinefs we value ourfelves fo much upon too—why, fure that and the linen manufacture are the only free trade we have.—O, here the company come.

Enter all the Company.

L. Kin. Well, where is this count, this hero of in- trigue?

O'Dogh. Below ftairs.

L. Bab. And in woman's clothes, Mr. Dogherty?

O'Dogh. And in woman's clothes, Lady Bab, come to make a cuckold of me; and if you will all hide yourfelves in the next room, you may fee how the operation proceeds— hufh—here he comes —get in, get in —and do not ftir—here he is—begone.

[*They all retire.—Exit O'Dogh.*

Enter KATTY, *and* MUSHROOM *in women's clothes.*

Katty. Step into this room for a moment, fir, and I will let my miftrefs know you are here—I proteft I fhould not have known you.

Mufh. Should not you? Ha, ha, ha! Why I think I do make a handfome woman, Mrs. Katty.

Katty. Handfome! why you are a perfect beauty! you are the very picture of a Connaught lady, that vifits my miftrefs—well, I will go and fee if the coaft is clear, and let her know you are come.

Mufh. Do, dear Mrs. Katty, and tell her my foul is all rapture, extacy, and tranfport, and rides upon the wings of love.

Katty. I will, I will, fir.   [*Exit.*

Mufh. A man muft fpeak nonfenfe to thefe creatures, or they will not believe he loves them. I fhall have more intrigues upon my hands in this country than I fhall know what to do with ; for I find the women all like me. As to Lady Kinnegad, I fee fhe is determined to have me.

L. Kin. Indeed! Conceited puppy!

Mufh. But fhe is grofs, coarfe, and ftinks of fweets intolerably.

L. Kin. Rafcal!

Mufh. Gazette is well enough ; I am fure I can have her. Yes, fhe's a blood, but fhe won't do above once and away.

Gazette. Saucy fellow!—but once indeed—I affure you!

Mush. Jolly has some thoughts of me too, I see—but she's an idiot, a fool—damned silly.

Mrs. Jolly. Mighty well, sir—very well—

Mush. But of all the spectacles that ever attempted to awaken gallantry, sure Nature never formed such another antidote as poor Lady Bab.

L. Bab. Oh the villain!—an antidote—an antidote—

Mush. She always puts me in mind of an old house newly painted and white-washed.

L. Bab. I will go tear his eyes out.

Mush. Then she is continually feeding that nose of hers, and smells stronger of rappee than Lady Kinnegad does of the Spice islands.

L. Kin. Oh, the rascal !

Mush. That Kinnegad is a damned tartar ; she and Mrs. Cardmark have fleeced poor Diggerty horridly —when I get Diggerty to England, I will introduce her to my lord ; for by that time I shall be tir'd of her. Oh, here the party comes.

Enter Mrs. DIGGERTY *and* KATTY.

My angel ! my goddess !

Mrs. Dig. O dear Mr. Mushroom, how could you venture so? I am ready to die with apprehension, left my husband should discover you.

Mush. Never fear, my charmer ; love despises all dangers, when such beauty as your's is the prize.

Mrs. Dig. But I hope, Mr. Mushroom, your passion is sincere ?

Mufh. Madam, the winged architect of the Cyprian goddefs has fabricated a pathetic ftructure in this breaft, which the iron teeth of Time can never deftroy.

Mrs. Dig. O dear Mr. Mufhroom, you are veeftly kind.

Katty. Come, come, madam, do you lofe no time, retire to your chamber, there you will be fafe, here you may be interrupted.

Mrs. Dig. Do you ftep and fend the fervants out of the way.

Mufh. Do, do, dear Mrs. Katty.

Katty. I will, I will.   [*Exit.*

Mufh. Dear creature, do but lay your hand upon my heart, and feel what an alarm of love and gratitude it beats.

[Katty *and* O'Dogherty *without.*

O'Dogh. Well, but Katty, if fhe is fo very ill, that is the very reafon why I muft fee her.

Mufh. Zounds ! your hufband's voice !

Mrs. Dig. O heavens !

Enter KATTY.

Katty. My mafter, my mafter !

Mrs. Dig. What will become of me ?

Katty. Run you down the back ftairs, madam, and leave him to me.

Mrs. Dig. Dear fir, farewell ; for heaven's fake, don't difcover yourfelf.

Mufh. No, no, madam, never fear me, not for the world.

Mrs. Dig. Adieu.   . [*Exit.*

Mufh. What the devil fhall I do, Mrs. Katty ?

Katty. Sit you ftill, fir, at all events—I will put out the candles. [*Puts them out.*] He will take you for my miftrefs ; pretend to be very ill ; leave the reft to me. Sure you can mimic a fine lady that has the vapours or the cholic.

Mufh. O nobody better !—nobody better—

Enter O'DOGHERTY *with a Piftol.*

O'Dogh. Heyday ! what in the dark, my dear ?

Katty. Yes, fir, my miftrefs is very ill, and cannot bear the light.

O'Dogh. What is her complaint ?

Katty. The cholic, fir.

O'Dogh. The cholic, fir! and what good can darknefs do the cholic, fir—get candles.

Mufh. Oh, oh !—no candles—no lights, pray my dear, no lights.

Katty. No, no lights—my lady has the head-ache, as well as the cholic, and the lights make her much worfe ; therefore, pray let her fit in the dark, fhe will foon be well—are you any better, madam ?

Mufh. A great deal, but no lights, pray—oh, oh, —no lights ! no lights !

O'Dogh. Well, my dear, you fhall have no lights, you fhall have no lights—leave us, Katty—I have

some bufinefs with your miftrefs. [*Exit* Katty.]
How are you, my dear? are you any better?

Mufh. Oh, a great deal, my dear.

O'Dogh. I am mighty glad of it, my foul. But
now, my dear, I have long wanted to have a little
ferious converfation with you upon a bufinefs that
has given me the utmoft uneafinefs, nay indeed the
utmoft torture of mind; fo without farther ceremony,
and in one word, to come to the point—I am jealous,
my dear.

Mufh. How! Jealous!

O'Dogh. Indeed I am, as are half the hufbands of
this town, and all occafioned by one man, which is
that coxcomb, Count Mufhroom.

Mufh. He is a very great coxcomb, I own, my
dear.

O'Dogh. You may fay that with a fafe confcience
—and a great jackanapes he is too into the bargain;
though, I muft own, the fellow has fomething gen-
teel in him notwithftanding.

Mufh. O yes, my dear, he is a very pretty fellow
—that all the world allows.

O'Dogh. It is very true, but his prettinefs will be
his ruin; for as he makes it his bufinefs and his
glory to win the affections of women, wherever he
goes, and as he has made conquefts of feveral mar-
ried women in this town, there are half a dozen huf-
bands of us that have agreed to poifon him.

Mufh. How! poifon him! O horrid! why that
will be murder, my dear.

H

O'Dogh. O that is none of our bufinefs---let him look to that---we muft leave that to the law---the fellow is always following you to the play-houfe, balls, and routs, and is conftantly fmiling at you, and ogling, and fighing---but if ever I catch him at thofe tricks again, as fure as his name is Mufhroom, I will put the lining of this little piftol into the very middle of his fcull.

Mufb Oh, oh, oh!

O'Dogh. He told me this morning that he had a new intrigue upon his hands this afternoon---I wifh I knew where it was; by all that's honourable, I would help the hufband to put eight or ten inches of cold iron into the rafcal's bowels.

Mufb. Oh, oh, oh!

O'Dogh. What is the matter, my dear? What makes you ftart and cry out fo? Give me your hand ---why you are all in a tremor! Ogho, why you have got the fhaking ague.

Mufb. I am mighty ill---mighty ill---

O'Dogh. Why you are all in a cold fweat---you had beft go up ftairs and lie down.

Mufb. No, no, no,---oh, no !---

O'Dogh. Why you fhall have fome immediate help---here, Katty---John---William---who's there?

Enter WILLIAM.

Will. Did your honour call, fir?

O'Dogh. Fly this minute to the next ftreet to Mr. Carnage the furgeon, and bid him haften hither to bleed my wife; then run as faft as you can to Doctor Fillgrave, and tell him my wife is very ill, and muft be bliftered directly.   Begone---fly---

Will I will, fir.   [*Exit.*

Mufb. Soh! what the devil fhall I do now. I fhall certainly be difcovered.   [*Afide.*

O'Dogb. How are you now, my dear?

Mufb. O better, better, a great deal.

O'Dogb. Oh, but for fear of the worft, I will have you bled plentifully, my dear, and half a fcore good roufing blifters laid on by way of prevention; for it is a very fickly time, my life.

Mufb. Aye, fo it is, my foul. But, my dear, I begin to be a little better; pray fend the maid hither.

O'Dogb. What do you want with the maid, my angel?

Mufb. I want her upon a particular occafion, my love—oh, oh, oh—

O'Dogb. Very well, my dear, I'll fend her to you. I think we have the count of the three blue balls in in a fine pickle; but I have not done with him yet. I have laid a ridiculous fnare for him, if he will but fall into it, that will not only expofe him to the world, but cure him for ever, I think, of trefpaffing upon matrimonial premiffes.   [*Exit.*

Mufb. Was ever poor devil fo fweated! I wifh I were out of the kingdom! I fhall certainly be poifoned among them! they are a damned barbarous people. I have often heard of the wild Irifh, but never believed there were fuch till now. Poifon a man, only for having an intrigue with a friend's wife.

Zounds, we never mind such things in England; but they are unpolished beings here.

Enter KATTY, *with two candles.*

Mush. Oh! Mrs. Katty, get me out of the house, or I am a dead man—he suspects I have a design upon his wife, and carries a loaded pistol to shoot me.

Katty. O heavens, sir—I don't know what to do with you—here comes my poor mistress, frighted out of her wits too.

Enter Mrs. DIGGERTY.

Mush. O, madam! if you don't contrive to convey me out of the house some way or other, I shall be detected, poisoned, shot, or run through the vitals.

Mrs. Dig. I am so distracted, I cannot think—you must even discover yourself to him, and say you came hither in that disguise out of a frolic.

Mush. Zounds, a frolic! Madam, he is as jealous as a Spanish miser, or an Italian doctor; he has a pistol in his pocket loaden with a brace of balls—he would shoot me, run me through the body, or poison me directly, should he discover me—have you no closet, or cup-board? Dear Mrs. Katty, cannot you contrive to get me out of the house in some shape or other?

Katty Why yes, fir, I have a contrivance that I think might fave you.

Muſh. What is it? what is it? quick, quick, for heaven's fake; for he certainly has a piftol in his pocket—he ſhewed it to me.

Katty. Why, fir, I have a large portmanteau trunk, by the help of which, I think, you might be fafely conveyed out of the houfe, if you would but fubmit to be ſhut up in it.

Muſh. Submit! zounds! any thing, any thing, dear Mrs. Katty, to fave my own life and a lady's honour. Why, child, it is an excellent contrivance, and, in my condition, perhaps the only one that could relieve me. For heaven's fake, let me fee it— where is it?

Katty. It ſtands juſt without the door here in the paſſage. [*Brings it in.*] Here it is, fir, if it is but big enough—that's all the danger.

Muſh. Zounds! let me try it—let me try it—quick —quick—put in my clothes—there—cram me in— buckle me up—ftay, ftay—leave this end a little open for air, or I ſhall be ſtifled—very well—excellent well—Mrs. Katty—there—cram me in—it will do— ſnug—ſnug—damned ſnug—

Mrs. Dig. Now call the men to carry it up to your room.

Katty. Here, John, William---

Servants [*Without.*] Madam.

Katty. Come here quickly.

Enter John *and* William.

Katty. Here take this portmanteau on your shoulders, and carry it up to my room—make haste.

[*The servants turn it up endways, with Mushroom's head to the ground, then raise it on their shoulders.*

Enter O'Dogherty.

O'Dogh. Where are you going with that portmantle?

John. Up to Mrs. Katty's room.

O'Dogh. Set it down here—what have you got in this portmantle, Katty?

Katty. It is, sir—it is—

O'Dogh. What, what is it?

Katty. Why it is—it is—

O'Dogh. Speak this minute, or I will put my sword up to the hilts in it.

Mush. Ah! Hold, hold— my dear Diggerty, hold —'tis I—'tis I—

O'Dogh. I—who the devil is I?

Mush. Mushroom—your friend Mushroom.

O'Dogh. What! Count Mushroom!

Mush. The same—the very same.—

O'Dogh. Hold the candle—aye, it is my friend the count indeed.

Mush. Zounds, my dear Diggerty—you have dropped the hot wax on my face.—do pray let me out.

O'Dogh. And so this was the new intrigue you told me of this afternoon.

Mush. Ah, my dear Diggerty, I was but in jest, upon my honour.

O'Dogh. Aye, now you are right, count—the intrigue was but in jest on my wife's side, indeed—here, ladies, come hither, and see this hero of intrigue and taste that they all admire so much.

Mush. Ah, dear Diggerty, don't expose me.

Enter the Company.

Omnes. Ha, ha, ha !

O'Dogh. Here, John—set him upon his legs on the ground—so—there—Lady Kinnegad, pray let me introduce you to the knight of the leathern portmantle.

L. Kin. Count, your most obedient—I would salute you, but I am coarse and stink of sweets.

Mush. Ah, my dear lady, that was only the wanton vanity of a coxcomb upon the verge of paradise as he thought.

Mrs. Jolly. Your humble servant, count—I would strive to extricate you, but, you know, I am an idiot, a fool—ha, ha, ha !

Mush. O dear Mrs. Jolly—

L. Bab. Yes, and I am like an old house newly

painted and white-wafhed, and I ftink of rappee. I
think a little rappee would not be amifs to clear your
eyes, and refrefh your fpirits, and there is fome for
you. [*Throws fnuff in his face*]

Mufb. O dear Lady Bab, this is [*Sneezes.*] cruel—
[*Sneezes.*] indelicate—[*Sneezes.*] and intolerable—
[*Sneezes.*] but I beg you will let me out of this con-
finement.

O'Dogb. Indeed I will not, for I intend that other
people fhall enjoy your fituation as well as I—this is
Lady High-Life's night—all the world is there—fo
here, John, take this portmantle on your fhoulders to
Lady High-Life's, with my compliments, and never
ftop till you take it up ftairs to the ball-room, and
there fet it down—they will be extremely glad to fee
their old friend, the count of the three blue balls.

Mufb. Mr. Diggerty—madam—ladies—

Omnes. Ha, ha, ha! away with him—away with
him.

Mufb. Mr. Diggerty, you fhall anfwer for this.

Omnes. Away with him—away with him. Ha,
ha, ha!   [*He is carried off.*

O'Dogb. Now, gentlemen and ladies, you may go
plunder one another at cards and dice as faft as you
can – and, like the count, make yourfelves objects.
for a farce.—If every fine lady and coxcomb in this
town were turned into a farce, faith we fhould be the
merrieft people in all Europe—but ours is over for
to-night, and pretty well upon the whole.

Indeed, I think 'tis very fairly ended :
The coxcomb's punish'd ;
The fine Irish lady's mended.

FINIS.

H 3

LOVE A-LA-MODE.

A

COMEDY.

BY CHARLES MACKLIN, ESQ.

ADAPTED FOR

THEATRICAL REPRESENTATION.

AS PERFORMED AT THE

THEATRES-ROYAL,

DRURY-LANE, COVENT-GARDEN, AND SMOCK-ALLEY.

REGULATED FROM THE PROMPT-BOOKS,

By Permission of the Managers.

"The Lines distinguished by inverted Commas, are omitted in the Representation."

DUBLIN:

PRINTED BY GRAISBERRY AND CAMPBELL,
FOR WILLIAM JONES, NO. 86, DAME-STREET.

M DCC XCIII.

LOVE A-LA-MODE.

ACT I. SCENE I.

Enter Sir THEODORE GOODCHILD *and* CHARLOTTE.

Sir Theodore.

WHAT will the world fay of me, but that I was a very prudent man ?

Char. The world ! The world will applaud you, efpecially when they know what fort of lovers they are, and that the fole motive of their affection is the lady's fortune. No poor girl fure was ever plagued with fuch a brood as I am—The firft upon my lift is a high-minded North Britifh knight, who fets up for a wit, a man of learning, and fentiment: He bears himfelf fair while you are prefent, but abufes the whole world when their backs are turned ; and withal, has fo high a notion of the dignity of his family, that he would, no doubt, think he laid me under a great obligation, in honouring me with his hand.—The fecond is a downright ideot, a fluttering, frivolous thing, well known in moſt public places by the name of Beau Mordecai, an Engliſh Jew.—The next in Cupid's train is your nephew, whoſe Iriſh voice and military aſpect make me fancy that he was not only born in a ſiege, but that Bellona alone could be his nurſe, Mars his preceptor, and the camp the academy, where he received the firſt rudiments of his education.

Sir Theo. My dear Charlotte! you ſhould not be ſo ſevere upon my nephew, what can you expect from a mere rough-hewn ſoldier, who muſt needs go from his friends a volunteer, and has lived theſe ſeveral years within the circuit of a camp; ſo that I don't believe he has ſix ideas diſtinct from his profeſſion.

Char. Let me ſee, his name is——

Sir Theo. Sir Callaghan O'Brallaghan.

Char. Sir Callaghan O'Brallaghan! It is enough to choak me——If I have him, I muſt have an Iriſh interpreter to make me underſtand what he ſays.

Sir Theo. Well, I muſt go and ſee about your ſuit; the coach waits——They all dine here, I think?

Char. All but Squire Groom, and he is to ride a match, which I ſuppoſe no charms could perſuade him to be abſent from.

Sir Theo. Well, make yourſelf what ſport you pleaſe with them——I ſhall certainly be back to dinner—Good morning to you, my dear.

[*Exit Sir* Theo.

Mordecai. [*Without.*] Sir Theodore, your ſervant— Is Miſs Charlotte this way?

Sir Theo. She is, fir—Good morning to you.

Mord. You'll dine with us, Sir Theodore?

Sir Theo. Certainly.

Enter Mordecai, *finging.*

Mord. Thus let me pay my softeft adoration, and thus, and thus, and thus, [*Kiffing her hand.*] In amorous tranfports breathe my laft.

Char. Not fo faft, Mr. Mordecai; you are very gallant, fir, and I proteft, I never faw you better dreft.

Mord. It is well enough, madam, juft as my taylor fancies: Do you like it?

Char. Oh! it is quite elegant; but, if I miftake not, you are fo remarkable for a tafte in drefs, that you are known all over the city, by the name of the Change-alley Beau.

Mord. They do diftinguifh me by that title, but I declare I have not the vanity to think I deferve it.

Char. Oh, Mr. Mordecai, well remembered! I heard of your amour at the opera with Mifs Sprightly.

Mord. Dear madam, how can you be fo fevere? That the lady has defigns, I ftedfaftly believe; but as for me——But pray, madam, who told you fo?

Char. Sir Archy Macfarcafm.

Mord. Oh, what a creature you have named! the very abftract of filth and naftinefs! He takes such a quantity of Scots fnuff, that he fmells worfe than a tallow-chandler's fhop in the Dog-days—There is

not one word of truth in five that he fays, and he ut-
ters his fimilies with all the gravity imaginable, after.
the moderate allowance of four bottles of port, three
ounces of Scots fnuff, and twelve pipes of tobacco.

Char. What a character has he drawn of the
knight!

Mord. Why, madam, I vow to Gad, he is the
daily fport of every coffee houfe in town; all his own
countrymen of any character conftantly avoid him,
and—Oh, the devil! here he comes.

Sir Archy. [*Without.*] Sawney, bid Donald bring
the chariot at aught o'clock exactly.

Enter Sir ARCHY MACSARCASM.

Mord. My dear knight, I am fincerely glad to fee
you, and have the honour, at all times, and upon
all occafions, to be your moft obedient humble fer-
vant.

Sir Archy. What, my child of circumcifion, how
do you do, my bonny Girgafhite? Gi'e us a wag
o' your luf, lad. Why, ye're as diligent in the fer-
vice o' your miftrefs as in the fervice o' your look-
ing-glafs; for your een or your thoughts are ay turn't
upo' the ane or the ither.

Mord. And your wit, I find, Sir Archy, like a
courtier's tongue, will always retain its ufual polite-
nefs.

Char. Civil and witty on both fides!—Sir Archy,
your fervant.

Sir Archy. Ten thousand pardons, madam—I did not observe you ; I hope I see your ladyship weel.— Ah! madam, you luik like a deeveenity. I see friend Mordecai is determined to bear awa' the prize frae us a' ; he's trickt out in a' the colours o' the rainbow.

Char. Mr. Mordecai is always well dress'd, Sir Archy.

Sir Archy. Upon my word he's as fine as a jay.— Step alang, man, turn round, and let us see your fine shape. Ah, he stands vera well, vera well indeed ! What's this in his hat ? A feather ! vera elegant, vera elegant I protest. I never saw a tooth drawer better drest a' my life.

Mord. Upon my word I am your most humble servant, Sir Archy.

Sir Archy. Weel, Mordecai, ye ha' been whispering your love-sick tale in the lady's lug, do ye ken that she is inclinable to your passion ?

Mord. From the conversation I have had with her, I begin to think that my figure and address have made an impression upon her.

Sir Archy. Vera weel, that's right, that's right—I mun ken that your ladyship has been entertain'd vera weel by my friend Mordecai, before I broke in upon you ; he's a gude ane at a tale, when the stocks is at ane end and the lottery at the ither, ha, ha, ha ! but ye maun ken that I ha' news for you that canna fail to gi' muckle sport.

Char. What is it pray, Sir Archy ?

Sir Archy. Why, ye maun ken that in my way to

your ladyſhip's manſion, I pickt up my, bonny Hibernian——as fine——upon my honour, as fine as little Mordecai here.

Char. But you have not left him behind you? I expected him here ere this.

Sir Archy. Left him! ye maun ken that I ha' brought him wi' me : for I'm like the monarchs of auld, I never travel without my fuil ; he is as good as a comedy or farce——But he has made a jargon, which he ſtiles a ſonnet, upon his bewitching Charlotte, as he calls you, madam ; he's now altering it, and ye maun expeck ſic an epiſtle, as has na been penn'd ſin' the days of Don Quixote. You have heard him ſing it, Mordecai ?

Mord. I beg your pardon, Sir Archy, I have heard him roar it.   Egad ! we have had him juſt now, madam, at a tavern, and made him give it us in an Iriſh howl, that might be heard from here to Weſt Cheſter.

Sir Archy. Why, Mordecai, you have a deeviliſh deal of wit, man ; aye, that's what ye hae.

Mord. Your moſt obedient, Sir Archy, I am afraid you flatter me ; but I muſt be going.—Madam, I kiſs your hand.

Char. You are not going to leave us, Mr. Mordecai ?

Mord. Only to have a ſlice of Sir Callaghan before dinner by way of a whet, that's all, madam, only by way of a whet.

Sir Archy. Not a word of the ſonnet, man ?

Mord. Never fear, Sir Archy, never fear.

[*Exit* Mord.

Sir Archy. What a fantaſtical baboon this little Iſraelite makes of himſelf!

Char. He is very entertaining, Sir Archy.

Sir Archy. The fallow's vera ridiculous, and therefore vera uſefu' in ſociety, for wherever he gangs there maun be laughter : But now, madam, a word or twa to our ain matters.——Madam, I love you, and gin I didna, I wad ſcorn to ſay it :——concerning theſe creatures who call themſelves your lovers, there are three of them about your ladyſhip's perſon, as unfit for you as a wandering Arab; and whaſe ſentiments are as wide o' true felicity as the north and ſouth poles : reptiles and beggars, wha can boaſt of naething, but a knowledge of ſic things as wad mak 'um be kend by a' judicious fok, e'en as the outcaſts o' the warld. And firſt this Mordecai, to be ſure the fellow's wealthy; yes he's wealthy—but then a reptile, madam, he's a reptile! whaſe common-place notions are o' nae farther extent than Change-alley, or the coffee-houſes, and whaſe only ideas are *cent. per cent.* ſchemes, ſtocks, annuities, and South Sea bubbles.

Char. Ay, Sir Archy! you are above ſuch groveling thoughts.—Your ambition is to adorn your mind.

Sir Archy. Then madam, as to Squire Groom : to be ſure he's a great ſportſman, but he's a beggar—a beggar! and nae doubt but your fortune would be very acceptable : 'twould enable him to redeem his ſtead o' horſes, put him on his legs again, and according till his ain phraſe, he would be bottom, madam, he would be bottom; but in a few years, madam, your whole fortune, the wiſe ſcraping of your anceſtors, would be wantonly ſquandered away upon cock-fighting, horſe-racing, grooms, jockeys, and ſic-like ſpendthrift amuſements ; and your ladyſhip not ha' a blanket left to cover you. Then, as to Sir Callaghan O'Brallaghan, the fellow's well enough to laugh at ; but ye maun luik about you there, for your guardian is his uncle, and to my certain knowledge, there is a deſign upon your fortune in that quarter : depend upon it, there is a deſign upon your fortune.

Char. I believe indeed, a lady's fortune is the principal object of every lover.

Sir Archy. I grant ye, madam, wi' Sir Callaghan O'Brallaghan, Squire Groom, and ſic-like fallows ; but men of honour have ither principles : I aſſure you, madam, 'tis not for the pecuniary, but for the divine graces o' your mind, and the mental perfections of your ſaul and body, which are more to me than all the riches of Peru and Mexico.

Char. O Sir Archy !

Sir Archy. Beſides, madam, gin ye marry me, ye will marry a man of ſobriety and economy. It is true, I am not in the hey-day of my blood, yet far from the vale of years, as the poet ſays. I am not like the young whipſters of this age, who are a' ſpirits at the firſt onſet, but gang aff like a ſquib, or a cracker on a rejoicing night, and are never heard o' mair. The young men now-a-days, madam, are mere baubles, abſolute baubles.

Char. Now, I think old men, Sir Archy, are but baubles.

Sir Archy. Beſides, madam, conſider the dignity

and antiquity of our family: madam, in our family there are three vifcounts, four barons, fix earls, feven marquiffes, and twa dukes: The families of the fouth are no to be compared to families o' the north.—— There is as muckle difference as between a hound of blood and a mongrel.

Char And why fo, fir?

Sir Archy. I'll tell you, madam—the nobeelity of Scotland are a' defcended frae renowned warriors, and heroes of glorious atchievements, wha difdain'd to mak alliances, or contaminate their bluid wi ony that war na as great as their ain.——But here in the fouth, ye o' the fouth, ye are a' fprung frae naething in the warld but wool packs, hop facks, fugar kifts, tar barrels, and rum puncheons.

Char. Ha, ha, ha!

Sir Archy. What gars you laugh, madam?

Char. The opinion you have of our nobility.

Sir Archy. Guide troth, madam, its true: a' we families of the north are of anither kidney quite: we difdain a mixture o' bluid that is na as pure as our ain; whereas ye are a ftrange amphibious breed, being a compofition of Turks, Jews, Nabobs, and Refugees.

Char. We are indeed a ftrange mixture, Sir Archy.

Sir Archy. Vera true, vera true;—my family is a family of rank and confequence; which, if ye marry into, will purify your bluid and refine it frae the lees and draps of trade, with which it is contaminated, which your money cannot do for you, war it as muckle as the bank of Edinbro'.

Enter Mordecai.

Mord. Sir Archy, he is juſt without, he is com·
ing.

Sir Callaghan O'Brallaghan. [*Without.*] Is the lady
this way do you ſay, young man ?

Servant. She is, ſir.

Sir Cal. Then I'll trouble you with no farther ce·
remony————

Enter Sir CALLAGHAN O'BRALLAGHAN.

Madam, I am your moſt obedient humble ſervant.

Char. I am very ſorry to hear we ſhall ſoon be de·
priv'd of your company, Sir Callaghan. I thought the
war in Germany had been all over.

Sir Cal. Yes, madam, it was all over, but it began
again——A ſoldier never lies in quiet, till he has no·
thing to do, then he quits the field with more ſafety.

Sir Archy. The lady was juſt ſaying, ſhe would be
glad if you would favour her with a ſlight narrative
of what happen'd in Germany.

Sir Cal. Pray, madam, don't ax me;—I am afraid
it would look like gaſconading in me ; and I will aſ·
ſure you there is no ſuch thing in nature, as giving a
deſcription of a fiery battle; for there is ſo much
done every where, that no body knows what is done
any where. Then, there is ſuch drumming and

trumpeting, and such delightful confusion altogether, that you can no more give an account of it, than you can of the stars in the sky.

Sir Archy. It's a very guid account he gi'es o't. [*Aside to* Mord.] Let us smoke him, and see if we can get a little fun with him —Try if he will give you some account of the battle.

Mord. Pray, Sir Callaghan, how many might you kill in any one battle you have been at ?

Sir Cal. [*Starting.*] I'll tell you—I generally kill more in a battle than a coward would chuse to look upon, or than an impertinent fellow would be able to eat. Are you answer'd, Mr. Mordecai ?

Sir Archy. You was devilish sharp upon him, faith.

Mord. Wasn't I ?

Sir Archy. Yes—but have another cut at him.— The Israelite will bring himself intil a damn'd scrape here. [*Aside.*]

Mord. Sir Callaghan, give me leave to tell you, if I was a general—

Sir Cal. A general ! Upon my soul, and you would make a fine general—Oh ! madam, look upon the general. Mr. Mordecai, do not look upon being a general as so light a matter. It is a very difficult trade to learn to be able to rejoice, with danger on the one side and death on the other, and a great many more things, that you know no more of, than I do of being high priest to a synagogue; so hold your tongue, my dear Mr. Mordecai, about that, and go mind your *cent. per cent.* and your lottery tickets in Change-alley.

I

Sir Archy. Ha, ha! by the Lord, he has tickl'd up the Ifraelite; he has given it to the Moabite on baith' fides o' the head.   [*Afide.*

Char. But you have been frequently in danger, fir?

Sir Cal. Danger, madam, is the foldier's profeffion; and death his beft reward.

Mord. A bull, a bull——Pray how do you make that out? You fay death is the foldier's beft reward.

Sir Cal. I'll tell you how—A general dead in the field of battle is a monument of fame, that makes him as much alive as Cæfar or Alexander, or any dead heroe of them all: and when the hiftory of America comes to be written, there is your brave young General Wolfe, that died in the battle before Quebec, will be alive to the end of the world.

Char. True, Sir Callaghan, the actions of that day will be remembered while Britain or Britifh gratitude have a name.

Sir Archy. Wha was it did the bufinefs at Quebec? Oh! the Highlanders bore the bell that day. Had you but feen them with their Andrewferraras, how they cut them, and flafh'd them about: they did the bufinefs, and gain'd immortal fame upon the fpot.

Sir Cal. Sir Archy, give me your hand: I affure you, your countrymen are brave foldiers; and fo are mine too.

Char. I think I hear Sir Theodore's coach ftop.

Enter Servant.

Serv. Madam, Sir Theodore waits for you, and dinner is almoft ready.

Mord. Madam, will you honour me with the tip of your wedding finger ?—Adieu, Sir Callaghan, Sir Archy, your fervant.—Adieu, Sir Callaghan.

[*Exeunt* Char. *and* Mord.

Sir Cal. A very impudent fellow this Mr. Mordecai ! if it had not been for the lady, I would have been a little upon the cavee with him.

Sir Archy. Becaufe the rafcal has been let into our company at Bath, he intrudes upon you wherever you go.—But have you written the letter to the lady ?

Sir Cal. Faith I have not ! for I thought it would not be right to make my addreffes to the lady, till I had made my affeions known to her guardian ; fo I have indited the letter to him.

Sir Archy. That's right, that's right ; for fo as ye do but right, it matters not to whom.—But where is it ?

Sir Cal. Here it is.

Sir Archy. I warrant it's a bonny epiftle.

Sir Cal. [*Reads.*] *Sir, as I have the honour to bear the charaer of a foldier, and to call Sir Theodore Goodchild uncle, I do not think it would be consiftent for a man of honour to behave like a fcoundrel.*——

Sir Archy. That's an excellent remark, an excellent remark, and vera new !

Sir Cal. [*Reads.*] *Therefore I thought proper before I proceeded any further, (for I have done nothing as yet) to open my mind to you before I gain the affeions of the lady.* You fee, Sir Archy, I was for carrying on my approaches like a foldier a la militaire, as we fay abroad. [*Reads.*] *You are senfible that my family is as old as any in the three kingdoms, and older too; I fhall therefore come to the point at once.* You fee I have given him a little rub by way of a hint about our family, becaufe Sir Theodore is a bit of a relation by the mother's fide only, which is a little upftart family that came in with one Strongbow t'other day, not above fix or feven hundred years ago: Now my father's family are all related to the O'Strickeffes, the O'Cannakans, the O'Callaghans, and I myfelf am an O'Brallaghan, which is the oldeft of them all.

Sir Archy. Yes, fir, I believe ye're of a vera ancient family, but ye're out in ane point.

Sir Cal. What's that, Sir Archy?

Sir Archy. Why fir, where ye faid, ye was as auld as ony family in the three kingdoms.

Sir Cal. Why then I faid no more than is true, Sir Archy.

Sir Archy. Hoot awa, man, ye dinna confider the families o' the north——Ye of Hibernia are as low as the bufhy bramble, and tuik refuge frae a' corners in that wild fpat whar ye live, penn'd up like a fet o' outcafts, and as fuch you remain until this hour.

Sir Cal. I beg your pardon, Sir Archy—that's the Scots account, which never fpeaks truth, becaufe it is partial—but the Irifh account, which muft be true, becaufe it is written by one of my own family, fays, the Scots are all Irifhmen's baftards.

Sir Archy. Baftards—what do ye make us illegitimate—illegitimate, fir?

Sir Cal. Why, little Terence Flaherty O'Brallagh-

an was the man who went over from Carrickfergus,
and peopled all Scotland with his own hands.

Sir Archy. Sir Callaghan, though your ignorance
and vanity would mak ravifhers of your anceftors, and
harlots and fabines of our mothers, yet ye fhall find
in me——

Sir Cal. Hark ye, Sir Archy, what was that you
faid juft now about ignorance and vanity?

Sir Archy. Sir, I denounce you baith ignorant and
vain, and mak your maift o't.

Sir Cal. Faith! I can make nothing at all of it,
becaufe they are not words that a gentleman is ufed
to; therefore you muft unfay them again.

Sir Archy. How, fir, eat my words, a North Briton
eat his words.

Sir Cal By my foul you muft, and that immedi-
ately.

Sir Archy. You fhall eat a piece of my weapon firft,
fir. [*Draws.*]

Sir Cal. Put up, for fhame, Sir Archy: confider
drawing a fword is a very ferious piece of bufinefs, and
fhould be done in private.

Sir Archy. Defend yourfelf—For, by the facred
crofs of St. Andrew, I'll have fatisfaction for making
us illegitimate.

Sir Cal. Now, by the crofs of St. Patrick, you are
a very foolifh man; but, if you have a mind for a
little of that game, come away to the right fpot.

Sir Archy. No equivocation, fir, dinna think you
have gotten beau Mordecai to cope with.

Sir Cal. Come on then for the honour of the fword:

——Oh ! you are as welcome as the flowers in May.

[*They fight.*

Enter CHARLOTTE.

Char. For heaven's fake, what's the matter ? what
is all this about ?

Sir Cal. It is about Sir Archy's great grand-mo-
ther, madam.

Char. Sir Archy's great grand-mother !

Sir Archy. Madam, he has caſt an affront upon a
hale nation, and I canna thole it.

Sir Cal. I am fure if I did it, it was more than I
intended : it was only to prove the antiquity of my
family.

Char. Pray, let me make peace between you.

Sir Archy. Sir, as ye fay ye didna intend the affront,
I am fatisfied.

Sir Cal. Sir Archy, there are two things I am al-
ways afraid of ; the one is of being affronted myſelf,
and the other of affronting any man.

Char. A very generous difpofition, Sir Callaghan
—but I hope this affair is over.

Sir Archy. I am fatisfied, madam ; but let me tell
you, Sir Callaghan, as a friend, as a friend, man,
you ſhould never enter into difputes about hiſtory, li-
terature, or antiquity of families, for you have got
ſuch a curfed wicked jargon upon your tongue——

Sir Cal Oh, I beg your pardon, Sir Archy—'tis
you have got ſuch a damn'd twiſt of Scots brogue,
that you don't underſtand good Engliſh when I ſpeak
it.

Sir Archy. Vera weel, vera weel—but you are out again ; for every body kens that I fpeak the footh country dialect fae weel, that wherever I gang I am always taken for an Englifhman—but we'll appeal to the lady which o' us twa has the brogue.

Sir Cal. With all my heart.—Pray, madam, have I the brogue ?

Char. No, fir.

Sir Cal. I am fure I never could perceive it.

Char. Neither have a brogue, you both fpeak very good Englifh—But come, gentlemen, dinner waits.

Sir Cal. We'll follow you, madam.

Char. Pray don't be long.   [*Exit* Char.

Sir Archy. Weel now, dinna gi'e o'er the defign of the letter.

Sir Cal. Sir Archy, never fear me, for as the old fong goes,

> *You never did hear,*
> *Of an Irifhman's fear,*
> *In love or in battle.*
> *In love or in battle.*
> *We're always on duty,*
> *And ready for beauty ;*
> *Tho' cannons do rattle.*
> *Tho' cannons do rattle.*
>
> *By day and by night*
> *We love and we fight,*
> *We're honour's defenders.*
> *We're honour's defenders.*

The foe and the fair,
We always take care
To make them surrender,
To make them surrender.

[*Exeunt.*

ACT II. SCENE I.

Enter Sir ARCHY MACSARCASM *and* CHARLOTTE.

Sir Archy.

WAUNS, madam! ſtep intil us for a few minutes; you will crack your ſides with laughing—We ha'e gotten anither fuil come to divert us unexpectedly, which I think the higheſt fuil that the age has produced.

Char. Who is it you mean, Sir Archy.

Sir Archy. Squire Groom, madam, the fineſt you ever beheld; in little boots half up his leg, a cap his jockey dreſs, and a' his pontificalibus, juſt as he made his match yeſterday at York. Antiquity in a its records of Greek and Roman folly never produced a senator visiting his mistress in so compleat a fool's garb.

Char. This is some new stroke of humour.

Enter MORDECAI.

Mord. Ha! ha! I shall burst :——I have left the Irishman and Squire Groom at a challenge.

Char. I hope not.

Sir Archy. Ha! ha! that is guid, that is guid : I thought it would come to action, ha! ha! that's clear!—we sal ha'e ane o' them pink'd.

Mord. O madam! the challenge need not terrify you : 'tis only in half pints of claret to your ladyship's health.

Char. Lord! Mr. Mordecai, how can you startle one so?

Sir Archy. I am very sorry for that : Guid troth! I was in hopes they had a mind to show their prowess before the lady their mistress, or that we should ha'e a little Irish or Newmarket bluid spilt. But what was the cause of the challenge, Mordecai?

Mord. Why, their passion for this lady——till the dispute rising high, they determined to decide it in a cascade of claret.

Char. Oh, I'm afraid they will kill themselves?

Sir Archy. Never fear, madam, nought's never in danger.

Mord. Look, look, the champion comes.

I 3

Enter Squire GROOM.

Groom Hoics, hoics!—hark forward my little princefs! forward, forward! hoics—Heaugh! madam, I beg a million of pardons for not being with you at dinner; it was not my fault, 'pon honour—I fat up all night, and propofed to fet out betimes; but about eleven o'clock laft night, at York—we were all damn'd jolly, and tofs'd off fix flafks of Burgundy a-piece. But that booby, Sir Roger Bumper, borrow'd my ftop watch to fet his by it.—Here it is, look at it, madam, it corrects the fun; they all go by it, madam, at Newmarket; and fo, madam, as I was telling you—the drunken blockhead put mine back two hours o' purpofe to deceive me, otherwife it was fifty to one, I could have been here to a fecond.

Char. Pray, fir, what is the meaning of this extraordinary drefs?

Groom. Not a peer in England could have one more tafty, the true turf tafte:—You muft know, madam, I rode my match in this very drefs yefterday, and Jack Buck, Roger Bumper, Frank Fudge, and a few more of them, laid me a hundred each, that I would not ride to London, and vifit you in it, ha! ha! but I've taken them all in damme; ha! ha! ha'nt I, madam?

Char. Pray, what time do you take to ride from York to London?

Groom. Ha! time, madam—why, bar a neck, a leg, or an arm, sixteen hours, seven minutes, and thirty-two seconds, sometimes three or four seconds under, that is, to the Stones, not to my own houfe.

Sir Archy. No, no, not till your ain houfe, that would be too much.

Groom. No, no, only to the Stones end; but then I have my own hacks, that are all steel to the bottom—all blood-stickers and lappers every inch of them, my dear, that will come through if they have but one leg out of the four. I never keep any thing, madam, that is not bottom—Game to the last! Game, ay, ay! you'll find every thing that belongs to me game!

Sir Archy. Weel faid, Squire Groom! Yes, yes, he is game to the bottom, he is game, madam.—There, walk about mon, and shew us your shapes; what a fine figure, and has fae guid an underftanding, that it's a pity he ever should do any thing but ride horfe-races.—What a fuil! don't you think he is a curfed ideot?   [*Afide to* Mord.

Mord. Well enough for a country fquire.

Groom. Well, madam, which of us muft be the happy man? You know I love you, madam—you know I do May I never crofs Joftle, if I don't.

Char. Oh, fir, I fee your paffion in your eyes.

Sir Archy. Weel, but fquire, you ha' gi'en us no account how your match went.

Char. What was your match, fir?

Groom. Our fubfcription and our fweepftakes.—There are feven of us, madam, Jack Buck, Lord Brainlefs, Bob Rattle—You know Bob, madam?—

Bob's a damn'd honeſt fellow——Sir Harry Idle,
Dick Riot, Sir Roger Bumper, and myſelf. We
put in five hundred pounds a-piece, all to ride our-
ſelves, and carry my weight—all to carry my weight:
The odds at ſtarting were ſeven to four againſt me
the field round ; and the field, ten, fifteen, and
twenty to one : For you muſt know, madam, they
thought they had me at a dead wind ; for the thing
I was to ride was let down in the back ſinews,
ha! ha! do you mind me, let down in his exer-
ciſe !

Sir Archy. Ah! that was unlucky.

Groom. Damn'd unlucky! but that my groom had
him gired, and he ſtood ſound, was in fine conditi-
on, ſleek as your ladyſhip's ſkin : We ſtarted off
ſcore, by Jupiter, and for the firſt half-mile you
might have cover'd us all with your under-petticoat.
I ſaw, I had them in hand, but your friend Bob,
madam, ha! ha! I ſhall never forget it : Poor Bob's
gelding took the reſt, flew out of the courſe, and
run over two attornies, a quack doctor, a methodiſt
parſon, an exciſeman, and a little beau, madam,
that you uſed to laugh at ſo immoderately at Bath—a
little dirty thing with a chocolate coloured phiz, juſt
like Mordecai.

Sir Archy. There he had the little Girgaſhite upon
the hip.

Groom. The people were in hopes he had killed the
lawyers, and were damnably diſappointed when they
found he had only broke the leg o' the one, and the
back of the other.

Char. Well, fir, pray inform us who won the fub-
fcription ?

Groom. It lay between me and Dick Riot, madam;
we were neck and heels for three miles, as hard as
we could lay leg to ground, and running every inch,
but at the firft I felt for him, found I had the foot—
knew my bottom—pull'd up—pretended to dig ;—but
Fudge—Frank Fudge gave the fignal to Tom Tickle-
purfe to lay it on thick : I had the whip hand all the
way—lay with my nofe in the neck under the wind
thus, fnug—fnug, my dear—had him quite in hand
——while Riot was digging and lapping right and
left, but it would not do, my dear, againft foot and
bottom and head.—I let go, darted by him like an
arrow—fo within a hundred yards of the diftance poft
poor Dick was blown to deftruction,. knocked up as
ftiff as a turnpike, and I left to canter in by myfelf,
madam, and I twitch'd them all round, grip'd the
gamblers, broke the blacklegs——for I took all the
odds before ftarting, fplit me! ha! was'nt I right,
old Shadrach ? ha ! took all the odds, took all the
odds, old dirt colour ?   [*To* Mord.

Sir Archy. Ha ! ha ! well, 'tis wonderful to think
at what a pitch of excellency our nobility are arrived
at in the art of fporting.   I believe we excel a' the
nobility of Europe in that fcience, efpecially in
jockeyfhip.

Groom. Sir Archy, I'll tell you what I'll do—I'll
ftart a horfe, fight a man, hunt a pack of hounds,
ride a match or fox chace, drive a fet of horfes, or
hold a toaft with any nobleman in the kingdom for a
thoufand each, and I fay done firft, damme.

Sir Archy. Ha! ha! the fquire's the keeneft
fportfman in a' Europe, madam.   There is naething
comes amifs to him, madam—he is a perfect Nim-
rod, he hunts a' things frae the flea in the blanket,
to the elephant in the foreft—he is at a' a perfect
Nimrod—are you not, fquire?

Groom. Yes—I am a Nimrod at all, at any thing.
Why I ran a fnail with his grace the other day for
five hundred pounds—there was nothing in it—won
it hollow, quite hollow !—half a horn's length.

Sir Archy. Half a horn's length! ah, that was hol-
low indeed.

Groom. Was it not hollow ?

Sir Archy. Oh, devilifh hollow indeed, Squire
Groom !—But where is Sir Theodore a' this time?

Groom. Oh! he's with Sir Callaghan, joking him
about drinking bumpers with me, and his paffion for
you, madam.

Sir Archy. You maun ken, gentlemen, this lady
and I have laid a fcheme to ha'e a little fport wi' Sir
Callaghan : If ye will a' ftep behin' the fcreen, I'll
gang and fetch him, and you fhall hear him mak love
as fierce as Alexander, or ony heroe in tragedy.

Groom. Sir Archy, I'll be as filent as a hound at
fault.

Sir Archy. Then, madam, do you retire and come
in till him, as if you came for the purpofe—I'll fetch
him in an inftant.

Sir Archy. I will be ready, Sir Archy.

[*Exit* Char.

Sir Archy. Get you behin' gentlemen—get you be-
hin'.   (*Exit Sir* Archy.

Groom! Ay, ay, we'll ſquat—never fear, Sir Archy—an Iriſhman make love!—I ſhall be glad to hear what an Iriſhman can ſay when he makes love. —What do you think he'll ſay, little Shadrach? Do you think he'll make love in Iriſh.

Mord. Huſh, huſh, ſquire! they are come.

          [They retire.

Enter Sir Archy *and Sir* Callaghan.

Sir Archy. Speak bawldly, man, ye ken the auld proverb—*Faint heart*—

Sir Cal. Oh, that's true,—*never won fair lady.* But you ſhall ſee, I will ſoon bring it to an ecclairciſſement.

Sir Archy. Oh, that's right, man, ſtick to that. She will be wi' you in a twinkling. I wiſh you guid ſucceſs,   *[Exit.*

Sir Cal. I will follow my friend Sir Archy's advice, and attack the dear creature with vigour at once. —Upon my conſcience, ſhe's here in the midſt of my ſoliloquy.

Enter Charlotte.

Char. Sir Callaghan, your's—I beg your pardon, I expected to find the other gentlemen here.

Sir Cal. Dear lady, your pardon you eaſily command; and as I am at war with the force of your charms, and mean to attack you inſtantly, will beg a truce before I come to action.

Sir. Archy. He begins vera weel—he has got intil
the heart of the battle already.

Char. But I am told, Sir Callaghan, you dedicate
some part of your time to the Muses, may I intreat
the favour of a song.

Sir Cal. Why, madam, I own I have been guilty
of torturing one of the Muses, in the shape of a song,
and I hope you'll excuse my putting your name to it.

Char. Upon condition that you will let me hear it.

Sir Cal. Oh ! dear madam, don't ask me, it's a
very foolish song—a mere bagatelle.

Char. Oh ! Sir Callaghan, I will admit of no ex-
cuse.

Sir Cal. Well, madam, since you desire it, you
shall have it, were it ten times worse—tol de rol, lol
—I don't know when I shall come at the right side of
my voice, tol, rol.

Sir Archy. Ha ! ha ! now for it—You shall hear
sic a sang as has na been penn'd sin' the days they first
clipt the wings o' the wild Irish.

Char. Dear sir, I am quite impatient

Sir Cal. Now, madam, I'll tell you before hand,
you must not expect fine singing from me as you hear
at the opera, because we Irishmen are not cut out for
it like the Italians.   [*Sings.*

Let other men sing of their goddesses bright,
Who darken the day and enlighten the night ;
I sing of a woman of such flesh and blood,
One touch of her finger would do your heart good.

Ten times in a day to her chamber I come,
To tell her my paſſion, but can't, I'm ſtruck dumb.
For Cupid he ſeizes my ſoul with ſurprize,
And my tongue falls aſleep at the ſight of her eyes.

Her little dog Pompey's my rival I ſee,
She kiſſes and hugs him, but frowns upon me :
Then pray, my dear Charlotte, debaſe not your
　　charms,
But inſtead of your lap-dog take me to your arms.

Sir Archy. Come now, the ſang's o'er, let us ſteal
awa'.

Groom. He's a damn'd droll fellow : Inſtead of
your lap-dog take me to your arms, ha! ha! ha!

Sir Archy. Huſh, ſaftly! dinna let him hear us
ſteal aff.—He's an excellent droll fellow, as guid as
a farce or a comedy—a deeviliſh comical cheel!
　　　　　　　　[*Exeunt Sir* Archy, Mord. *and* Groom.

Char. But, Sir Callaghan, I fear no lady can boaſt
of allurements, ſufficient to make you quit the army.

Sir Cal. Why, madam, when in my very early
years, my good king was my friend in diſtreſs, and
now he's at war, and wants my aſſiſtance, I ſhould
be a poltroon to leave him.

Char Why then, Sir Callaghan, your ſervant,
War is your miſtreſs, and to her charms I reſign you.
　　　　　　　　　　　　　　[*Exit* Char.

Sir Cal. Upon my conſcience I feel very fooliſh—
Oh, but I will make a general attack, give the *coup*
de main, raiſe the ſiege, ſet off for Germany to-mor-

row morning—tell her my paffion, and take my leave
without faying a word.

Enter Sir ARCHY *and* MORDECAI.

Mord. Why, Sir Archy, from what I can at pre-
fent perceive, by the dejected looks of Sir Theodore,
the lady herfelf, and in fhort the behaviour of the
whole family, certainly fomething wrong in their af-
fairs has juft happened.

Sir Archy. Your conjectures are very right, Mr.
Mordecai—'tis a' over with him—he's an undone
beggar, and fae is the girl.

Mord. Sir, you aftonifh me.

Sir Archy. 'Tis an unexpected bufinefs, but it's a
fact, I affure you. Here he is himfulf, poor devil,
how wae he looks !

Enter Sir THEODORE *and a* LAWYER.

Sir Theo. This unexpected blow from abroad af-
fects me indeed : What, my friend to fail me in
whom I placed fuch an implicit faith ! Not only to
venture my own, but unfortunately my dear girl's for-
tune. Her misfortunes touch me more than my
own ; however, I will endeavour to bear this fhock
as well as I can, collect my fpirits, and break this
affair to my poor Charlotte.

[*Exeunt Sir* Theo. *and Lawyer.*

Mord. Fore gad, this is furprifing ! Sir Archy, what has occafioned all this ?

Sir Archy. Faith, Mordecai, I dinna ken the particulars : but it feems by the words of Sir Theodore himfelf, a rich merchant in Holland his partner, and he—the guardian over this lady, are both bankrupts ; and as the lawyer there without confirms, have failed for above an hundred thoufand pounds more than they can anfwer.

Mord. And how does that affect the young lady ?

Sir Archy. Why, fir, the greateft part of her fortune it feems was in trade with Sir Theodore—befides the fuit in Chancery for above forty thoufand has been determined againft her this very day, fo that they are a' undone.

Mord. You furprife me, Sir Archy, I thought the forty thoufand was proved clearly in her favour.

Sir Archy. O ye dinna ken the law ; the law is a fort of Hocus Pocus, that fmiles in your face although it pick your pocket ; and the glorious uncertainty of it is of more ufe to the profeffors than the juftice of it. Here they come, and feemingly in great affliction.

Enter *Sir* Theodore *and* Charlotte.

Char. My dear guardian and parent, let me call you, for indeed fuch you have ever been, give not yourfelf up to grief on my account.

Sir Theo. It is only on your account that I can be miferable, and yet for you there is a beam of hope :

I think we can with fafety rely upon the honour and integrity of Sir Archibald Macfarcafm, who will marry and fnatch you from all misfortunes.

Sir Archy. Gin ye rely upon me, ye rely upon a broken ftaff ; ye may as well rely upon the philofopher's ftane.   What ? would you marry me to make me a mender of broken citizen's fortunes ; but I'll fpeak to them, and end the difpute at anes.——I am concern'd to fee you in this diforder, Sir Theodore.

Char. Oh ! Sir Archy, if all the vows you ever profefs'd and fo lavifhly beftow'd, were real, I am fure this change of fortune will make no alteration in your fentiments of honour.   Now let the truth be feen.

Sir Archy. Madam, I am forry to be the meffenger o' ill news, but a' our connections is at an end. Our houfe has heard o' my connections wi' you, and I have had letters frae fix dukes, five marquiffes, four earls, three barons, and other dignitaries o' the family, remonftrating, nay exprefsly prohibiting my contaminating the bluid of the Macfarcafms wi' any thing fprung frae a hogfhead or a compting houfe. I affure you, madam, my paffion for you is vera ftrong, but I canna bring difgrace upon an honourable family.

Char. There is no truth, no virtue in man.

Sir Archy. Guid troth, nor in woman neither that has nae fortune ! Here is Mordecai, a wandering Ifraelite, a vagabond Hebrew, that's a very cafualty, fprung frae annuities, bulls, bears, and lottery tickets, and can hae nae family objections—he is paffionately fond o' you, and till this offspring of accident and Mammon I refign my intereft in ye.

Mord. I beg your pardon, Sir Archy, I beg your pardon ; marriage is a thing I have not thoroughly confider'd, and I muft take fome time before I can determine upon fo inextricable a fubject, and I affure you, madam, my affairs at prefent are not in a matrimonial pofture.

Char. I defpife both them and you.

Enter Sqaire Groom.

Groom. Hoicks, hilli ho, ho !—why what's the matter here ? what are we all at fault ? Is this true, Sir Theodore ? Zounds, I hear that you and the filly both run o' wrong fide the poft.

Sir Theo. Squire this is no time to joke and trifle, or to attempt to difguife our feelings on fo ferious and affecting a ftroke. However, fir, this is a charming girl, whofe virtues deferve a noble fortune, but the lofs of it will furely make no abatement in your affections.

Groom. Harkye, Sir Theodore, I always make a match agreeable to the fpeed or age of my cattle, or the weight my things can carry. When I offer'd to match her give and take, the filly was neither piper nor blinker—cheft bound nor fpavin'd ; but I hear now her wind's touch'd ; if fo I would not back her for a fhilling. I'll take her into my ftead, if you will —fhe has a fine forehand—fhe moves her pafterns well, gets on a good pace, a deal of fafhion and fome

blood, and will do well enough to breed out of; but
I won't keep her in training though, for fhe can't carry
weight enough to come thro'—Matrimony, fir, is a
curfed long courfe, devilifh heavy and fharp turnings ;
it won't do—fhe can't come thro'—no, damme, fhe
can't come thro' !

Sir Archy. I think, fquire, ye judge right in my
thoughts—the beft thing the lady can do, is to fnap
at the Irifhman.

Mord. Well obferved, Sir Archy.

Groom. Ay, ay, Archy has an excellent nofe, and
hits off a fault as well as any hound I ever follow'd.

Sir Archy. He's fic a luiver as a lady in her cir-
cumftances could wifh.

Char. Thou wretch, whofe fentiments of honour
are ftill more defpicable than your fentiments of love !
though I am to fortune loft, my mind fhall never be
guilty of principles of bafenefs.

Mord. Hufh, hufh ! he's here.

Enter Sir CALLAGHAN.

Sir Archy. What, my guid friend, Sir Callaghan,
I kifs your hand.   I ha' been fpeaking to the lady in
your behalf wi' a' the eloquence I ha'—fhe is ena-
mour'd of your perfon, and ye are juft come in the
nick o' time to receive her heart and hand.

Sir Cal. 'Pon my confcience, Sir Archy, I fhould
be prouder to receive that lady's hand than a general's
ftaff, or the greateft honour the army could beftow
upon me.

Sir Archy. 'Twould be a devilish lucky match for her.—The fellow has a guid fortune, is a great blockhead, and loves her vehemently—three excellent qualities!—Come, come, madam, true love is impatient and despises ceremony—gi'e him your hand at anes.

Char. No, sir, I cannot impose myself upon Sir Callaghan as unworthy of his esteem, and destitute of friends and fortune.

Sir Cal. What means all this?

Sir Theo. Why nephew, this lady here, my unfortunate ward, this morning was possess'd of a legacy, as we thought, fit to make happy the first of families, but by my ill conduct and want of care, her fortune which I had ventur'd in trade is lost abroad, and the law suit lost at home—Therefore her virtue, not fortune, must now be the object of your affections.

Sir Cal. I assure you, Sir Theodore, I rejoice at her distress—for when she was rich I approach'd her with fear and trembling, because I was not her equal: But now she is poor and has nobody to defend her, I feel something warm about my heart, that tells me I love her better than when I thought she was rich; and if my life and fortune will be of any service to her, she shall command them for ever and ever.

Char. Generous man!

Sir Theo. And will you take her for life?

Sir Cal. Ay! and for death too, which is a great deal longer than life you know.

Sir Theo. Then take her, sir, and with her an ample fortune—my bankruptcy was entirely feign'd—it

was only to try the sincerity of these gentlemen who
call themselves lovers.

Mord. How's this?

Groom. A hellish cross flung upon us by heavens—
distanc'd to damnation.

Sir Arch. Gently, gently, whisht—he's only taking
him in—the bubble's bit.

Sir Theo. Why do you now pause, dear nephew?
It was only a scheme to try the mean, the mercenary,
illiberal arts of those who are a disgrace to mankind,
their country and themselves.

Sir Cal. Why this is something like what those lit-
tle jackanapes about town call humbugging a man.—
First, she has no fortune, then she has a fortune, and
then she has no fortune again.

Sir Theo. What I now tell you is a sacred truth.
Take her, sir, and with her a heart worthy your ac-
ceptance—take her as a reward for your disinterested
affection.

Sir Cal. Take her—the devil take me if I don't.

Char. And I yield to your proposal with unfeigned
pleasure.

Sir Cal. By the glory of a soldier, I had rather be
at her foot than at the head of a regiment—and now
she's mine by all the rules of war, I have a right to
lay her under contribution, for her kisses are lawful
plunder. [*Kisses her.*] O ye are a little tight crea-
ture!—'Pon honour, her breath is as sweet as the
sound of a trumpet.

Groom. Why the knowing ones are all taken in
here—stripp'd and double distanc'd. Zounds, the
filly has run a crimp upon us.

Mord. Damn it, fhe has jilted us moft confound-
edly.

Sir Archy. By the crofs of St. Andrew, I'll be re-
venged.—I ken a lad of an honourable family, wha
underftands the ancient claffics in a' perfection—He
is now compofing a comedy, and he fhall infinuate
baith their characters intil it.

Mord. And I'll write a lampoon, where fhe fhall
have an intrigue with a life-guards-man, a grenadier,
and an opera finger.

Groom. I have a hedge yet. I can't write, but I'll
tell you what I'll do—I'll poifon her parrot, kill her
monkey, and cut off her fquirrel's tail, damme.

Sir Cal. Harkye, gentlemen, I hope you'll afk my
leave for all this. If you offer to write any of your
nonfenficals, or if you offer to touch a hair of the
parrot's head, or a feather of the monkey's tail, or a
hair of any thing belonging to this lady, I'll be after
making a few remarks upon your bodies. Look ye,
I have an excellent pen by my fide that is a good cri-
tic, and writes a legible hand upon impertinent au-
thors.

Sir Archy. Hoot awa', hoot awa', man, dinna talk
in that idle manner, fir. Our fwords are as fharp and
as refponfible as the fwords of ither men ; but this is
nae time for fic matters ; ye hae got the lady, and we
ha'e got the willow. I am only forry for the little
Girgafhite, beau Mordecai, for he has befpoke the
nuptial chariot and a' his liveries ; and my friend
Squire Groom, I fear is quite lock'd in wi' the turf ;
—and guid troth I am forry for the lady, for fhe has

loſt being match'd into the great houſe of the Mac-
ſarcaſms, which is the greateſt loſs of a'.

Sir Cal. This is ſomething like the cataſtrophe of a
ſtage play, where knaves and fools are diſappointed.

Sir Theo. And an honeſt man rewarded.

F I N I S.

THE

GOVERNESS.

A

COMIC OPERA.

BY R. B. SHERIDAN, ESQ.

ADAPTED FOR

THEATRICAL REPRESENTATION.

AS PERFORMED AT THE

THEATRES-ROYAL,

DRURY-LANE, COVENT-GARDEN, AND

SMOCK-ALLEY.

REGULATED FROM THE PROMPT-BOOKS,

By Permission of the Managers.

DUBLIN:

PRINTED BY GRAISBERRY AND CAMPBELL,
FOR WILLIAM JONES, NO. 86, DAME-STREET.

M DCC XCIII.

DRAMATIS PERSONÆ.

Men.

Enoch Issachar,	- - -	Mr. Ryder.
Don Pedro,	- - -	Mr. Vandermere.
Octavio,	- - -	Mr. Owenson.
Sancho,	- - -	Mr. G. Dawson.
Father John,	- - -	Mr. Wilder.
Lorenzo,	- - -	Mr. Du Bellamy.

Women.

Ursula, *the Governess*,	- -	Mrs. Heaphy.
Flora,	- - -	Mrs. Thompson.
Sophia,	- - -	Miss Potter.

Friars, Masks, Servants, &c.

GOVERNESS.

ACT I. SCENE I.

Enter SANCHO, *with a lanthorn.*

Sancho.

WELL, furely, this is the hardeft tafk in nature, to ferve a man fo far gone in love.—Why, my mafter neither eats, drinks, nor fleeps; and here I am obliged to attend him, night and day, in the charming amufements of fafting and waking :—This may be pleafant to a lover; but as I am not one of the fighing gentry, I could wifh for more fubftantial entertainment.—At this rate, we fhall make a black lent of the whole year :—in a fortnight I fhall be fhrunk to lefs than a fizeable eel ;—my cheeks are already thinner than parchment, and my jaws, for want of proper ufe, are almoft lock'd :—This mafter of mine, is—but, here he comes.

Enter LORENZO.

Loren. Well, firrah, what are you doing here? Did I not order you home?——

San. I was thinking, fir, if you would but be perfuaded to go home, lay down, and take a little bit of a nap—if it was but by way of novelty, it——

Loren. Who bid you think, rafcal? Begone! and let me no longer be troubled with your impertinence.

San. Impertinence! Dear fir, confider my melancholy condition; and, if you will indulge any paffion, pray let it be compaffion for the hollow found of my ftomach——

Loren. Peace, cormorant! Thou haft not an idea beyond the grofs fenfation of eating.

San. I confefs the charge, and heartily wifh it more fubftantial than mere idea.——

Loren. No more, dolt! You fhall faft and wake as long as I pleafe;—fo begone home, as you fear correction.   [*Exit* Loren.

San. There he goes! Love has taken full poffeffion of his brain; and until he comes to his fober fenfes, I fhall have neither food nor reft. Plague of all your fine fenfations, I fay.   [*Exit* San.

Enter OCTAVIO, LORENZO, *and gentlemen, with guittars, and maſk'd; who approach under* Sophia's *window.*

SERENADE.

Octav. *Tell me, my lute, can thy fond ftrain,*
        So gently fpeak thy mafter's pain,

So softly sing, so humbly sigh,
That—tho' my sleeping love shall know
Who sings—Who sighs below,—
Her rosy slumbers shalt not fly.

Thus may some vision whisper more,
Than ever I dare speak before!

Lor. 'Tis all in vain, Octavio; Sophia will not hear
you; and, if she does, 'twill be to little purpose.

Octav. I am not of your opinion, Lorenzo: a sin-
cere and tender lover should never shrink at a faint
repulse: if she is within hearing, I doubt not to con-
vince you of your error.

A I R.

Octav. The breath of morn bids hence the night ;
Unveil those beauteous eyes, my fair ;
For, till the dawn of love is there,
I feel no day—I own no light.

[*After the song* Sophia *appears at her window.*]

A I R.

Sophia. *Waking, I heard thy numbers chide,*
Waking, the dawn did bless my sight :
'Tis Phœbus sure that wooes, I cry'd,
Who speaks in song, who moves in light.

[*Don Pedro above—opens his window.*

A I R.——TRIO.

Don Pe. What vagabonds are these I hear,
Fiddling, fluting, rhyming, ranting,
Piping, scraping, whining, canting?
Fly, scurvy minstrels, fly!

Sophia. Nay, prithee, father, why so rough?

Oct. An humble lover I!

Don Pe. How durst you daughter, lend an ear
To such deceitful stuff?
Quick from the window fly!

Sophia. Adieu, Octavio!——Oct. Must you go?

O. & S. We soon, perhaps, may meet again;
For tho' hard fortune is our foe,
The god of love will fight for us.——

Don Pe. Reach me the blunderbuss!

O. & S. The god of love who knows our pain.

Don Pe. Hence, or these slugs are thro' your brain.

SCENE II.

Chamber in Don Pedro's *house.—Enter* DON PEDRO
and SOPHIA.

D. Pe. 'Tis well the catterwauling puppy made his

escape :—a minute more, and I would have made a
riddle of his callicoe carcase.

Soph. Why, sir, should his honourable love subject
him to such cruel treatment ?

D. Ped. Honourable love ! and cruel treatment ?—
fine romantic babble, truly !—But I'll make you
know, sighing, whining madam, that you are a daugh-
ter born to obey, and I a father, born to command,
—absolute in power, and shrewd in discernment :—
so, no more tricks, d'ye hear ?—

[Exeunt into the house.

SCENE III.

Street.—Enter LORENZO *and* OCTAVIO.

Oct. Nay, prithee don't be grave, Lorenzo—I have
my perplexities ; yet bear up against them.

Lor. I am the most unfortunate of all men living,
Octavio—

Oct. What is the matter ?—Has Flora and you had
any difference ?

Lor. I am on the rack !—She is so much displeas-
ed, that I know not if ever I shall see her again.

Oct. What, has she taken ill ?—You must have been
much to blame ; for Flora is all gentleness.

Lor. Indeed I found it was impossible to attempt
seeing her, the father kept so watchful an eye :—so

that I attempted to bribe her maid, which fucceeded
to my wifh, and fhe conveyed me to her apartment.

Oct. A gallant youth, upon my word!—And,
then, I'll be fworn you took fome liberty that has
fhocked her delicacy.—Tell me, did you dare to take
her hand?

Lor. Moft affuredly I did.

Oct. And did you prefume to trefpafs on a kifs,
without her confent?

Lor. A kifs!—I ravifhed a dozen from her.—

Oct. And can you wonder at her difpleafure?

Lor. Not in the leaft: but I am diftracted in hav-
ing loft her.

A I R.

Lor.	*Could I her faults remember,*
	Forgetting ev'ry charm,
	Soon would impartial Reafon
	The tyrant Love difarm:
	But when enrag'd I number
	Each failing of her mind,
	Love ftill fuggefts her beauty,
	And fees, while Reafon's blind.

Lor. Octavio, you were once fond of Flora: how
ftands your affection now?

Oct. Your fifter now poffeffes all my foul.—I once
thought Flora had charms; but the coldnefs and ne-
glect with which fhe treated me, recalled my heart to
its wonted ftate of indifference.

AIR.

Oct.   *I ne'er could any lustre see*
   In eyes that would not look on me :
   I ne'er saw nectar on a lip,
   But where my own did hope to sip.
   Has the maid who seeks my heart
   Cheeks of rose untouch'd by art ?
   I will own the colour true,
   When yielding blushes aid their hue.

   Is her hand so soft and pure ?—
   I must press it to be sure :
   Nor can I e'en be certain then,,
   'Till it grateful press again.
   Must I, with attentive eye,
   Watch her heaving bosom sigh ?
   I will do so—when I see
   That heaving bosom sigh for me.

Lor. I'll do all in my power to assist your suit with
my sister :—but I charge you not to attempt running
away with her.—You shall have my interest as far as
that can serve you.

Oct. Would not you, Lorenzo, run away with Flora,
if she would consent ?

Lor. I must confess I should not hesitate : but, you
will allow, we never do by other men's wives and
daughters, as we wish they should do by our's.

Oct. You need be under no uneasiness, on my ac-
count, in respect to Flora.

AIR.

Oct.   *Friendship is the bond of reason;*
      But, if beauty disapprove,
      Heav'n absolves all other treason,
      In the heart that's true to love.

      The faith, which to my friend I swore,
      As a civil oath I view:
      But to the charms which I adore,
      'Tis religion to be true.

      Then if to one I false must be;
      Can I doubt which to prefer—
      A breach of social faith with thee,
      Or sacrilege to love and her.

                    [*Exit* Oct.

Lor. Sure Octavio has no lurking passion for Flora.
And yet, methinks, this change may be all pretence:
for who that has ever loved her can cease to do so—
But, from his try'd sincerity, how can I doubt his
friendship?

AIR.

Lor.   *Tho' cause for suspicion appears,*
      Yet proofs of her love too are strong:—
      I'm a wretch if I'm right in my fears,
      And unworthy her smiles if I'm wrong.
  What heart-breaking torments from jealousy flow,
  Ah! none but the jealous—the jealous can know!

When bleß with the smiles of my fair,
I know not how much I adore ;
These smiles let another but share,
And I wonder I priz'd them no more:
Then whence can I hope a relief from my woe,
When the falser she seems, still the fonder I grow !

[*Exit* Lor.

SCENE IV.

Chamber in Don Pedro's house.—*Enter* Sophia *and*
Governess.

Gov. Are you still determined, my dear miss, to
take so rash a step?—Are you really so fond of Oc-
tavio, as to marry him without a fortune ? I fear you
will hereafter repent, and reflect on the imprudence
of your choice.

AIR.

Soph. *Thou can'st not boast of fortune's store,*
        My love ! while me they wealthy call ;
      But I was glad to find thee poor—
        For, with my heart, I'd give thee all,
      And then the grateful youth shall own,
      I lov'd him for himself alone.

But, when his worth my hand shall gain,
No word or look of mine shall shew
That I the smallest thought retain
Of what my bounty did bestow :
Yet still his grateful heart shall own,
I lov'd him for himself alone.

Gov. Indeed, Sophia, I overheard your father say, you should marry little Enoch the Jew to-morrow morning :—Now, if we succeed in our plot, you shall give him up to me entirely.

Soph. O, yes, with all my heart !—But have you gained the maid to my interest ?—My brother Lorenzo has promised his assistance.

Gov. All is as you wish.—But I must have Octavio's last letter : that must be the cause of his suspicion ; and leave the rest to me.

Soph. There it is ; [*Gives a letter.*] and I wish you success with all my heart.

Enter DON PEDRO *and* LORENZO.

Don Ped. What is all this scraping, fiddling, and serenading !—I desire I may have no more of it.—And what have you been about, sir ?—disturbing some honest family in the same manner, I suppose ! Sophia, to-morrow, child, I have determined you shall marry Enoch Issachar ; and then—

Soph O, sir, do not make me miserable !—

D. Ped. Any thing more ?

Soph. Sir, he's a Jew—

D. Ped. That's a miftake : for he has changed his religion thefe fix weeks.—Any thing more ?

Soph. Sir, he's a Portuguefe.

D. Ped. That's another miftake; for he has forſworn his country.—Any thing more ?

Soph. Sir, he has, to me, the greateft fault that ever a man had.

D. Ped. Hey-day !—What's that, pray ?

Soph. He is my averfion.

D. Ped. Sophia, I care not : I know he loves you, and has the money. The beft experiment in nature, to obtain good fruit, is to graft on a crab.—You know, my wife and I lived very happy; yet there was no love between us, and we expected none; therefore, were not difappointed :—and, the poor woman, when fhe died, I was fo forry, that I did not care if fhe had lived. I wifh every man in Spain could fay as much. And now, fir, if you have any more advice to give your fifter, about difobedience to her father, be brief; for I intend to lock her up in her room, and will not fee her face, till fhe returns to her duty.

Lor. Sir, for my fifter's fake, I cannot help fpeaking—

D. Ped. Then, fir, for my fake, hold your tongue.

[*Exit* Lor.

[Don Pedro *locks up* Sophia, *and, returning, meets the* Governefs.

D. Ped. So, madam ! have I found you out !—Here's a witch ! engaged in Octavio's intereft. How did you dare to encourage fuch a piece of mifchief ?

Gov. Well, and if I am in Octavio's interest, I am
not ashamed to own it ; for I always delighted in the
tender passions—

D. Ped. In the tender passions ! O, you old piece of
antiquity, you are an antidote to all the tender passi-
ons.   Get out of my house, this moment, out of my
house, I say !—you, that I took into my house to be
a scare-crow, to become a decoy-duck !—Get along !
you old piece of iniquity !

Gov. Well, sir, I don't want to stay in your house ;
but I must go and lock up my wardrobe.

D. Ped. Your wardrobe !   When you came into my
house, you could carry your ward-robe in your comb-
case, you could, you old dragon !

Gov. And my veil, too—I hope you would not have
me go without my veil.

D. Ped. Your veil !   you can't go without a veil,
indeed !—I suppose you are afraid of your beauty.
Well go along and get your veil, you old devil :. [*He
lets the* Governess *into* Sophia.]   A fine story indeed !
if parents are to be disobeyed on account of love,
liking, beauty, and such nonsense :—But, as my fa-
ther made me marry to please him, without caring two-
pence for my bride ; so, my daughter shall marry to
please me, though age, deformity, and avarice should
be my choice.

A I R.

If a daughter you have, she's the plague of your life :
No peace you shall know—tho' you've buried your wife :

At twenty she mocks at the duty you taught her.
O ! what a plague is an obstinate daughter !
　　Sighing and whining !
　　Dying and pining.
O ! what a plague is an obstinate daughter !

When scarce in their teens they have wit to perplex us,
With letters and lovers for ever they vex us ;
While each still rejects the fair suitor you've brought her,
　　Wrangling and jangling !
　　Flouting and pouting !
O ! what a plague is an obstinate daughter !

D. Ped. So, madam, you have got your veil :—
now march off;—and, if you please, I'll see you clear
of my house.—There, go—go to Octavio !—go to
him ;—and, do you hear ?—since he has got you
turned out of a good place, he had better make you
amends, by taking you home with himself.

　　　　　　　　　　　　[*Exit* Don Pedro.

SCENE V.

Enter Sophia, *who peeps through her veil.*

Soph. Good bye to you, sir.　　　　[*Laughing.*

Flo. Won't it be dangerous if he sees you ?

Soph. No, my dear, he never saw me ; but his frequent visits to my father's made him shew his odious figure very often before my window, from whence he was shewn to me.

Flo. He comes this way : I'll leave you : [*Going*] —But, Sophia, when you see your brother, be sure you don't tell him that I am gone to the convent of St. Catharine's, two doors down, on the right hand side of the piazza.

Soph. Oh, you may depend upon it, I will tell him where you may not be found : [*Going.*] But, my dear friend, will you allow me to make use of your name, as I may find occasion.

Flo. With all my heart ;—any thing in my power you may command.   [*Exit Flora.*

Enter ENOCH.

En. Ay, ay, !—there's no doubt this little figure of mine will soon captivate the heart of Don Guzman's daughter.—But, who have we here ?—a pretty girl, faith !—how she eyes me : [*She approaches.*] Ay, ay ! she is certainly struck with my dress and figure : and I don't wonder at it ;—I have some reason to think they are particularly striking.——

Soph. Sir, your servant :—good stranger, I hope you will excuse this liberty ;—I have a favour to request of you.——

En. I am sorry for you, young woman ;—but I am positively engaged——

Soph. But, sir, you don't seem to underftand me—

En. I can't make you any honourable propofals ;— and, if I was to offer any thing elfe, I fuppofe you have fome good-natured brother or coufin, that would run me through the guts.—You have no hopes, child ;——I am forry for you.

Soph. It is not your perfon I folicit ; I have no ambition of that kind ; my fuit is of a very different nature : To be plain with you, fir, I am told you are acquainted with Signor Octavio ;—if it is not too much trouble, and you will lend your pity to a ftranger, pleafe to direct him to me.

En. Oh,—then 'tis not me you are fond of ?——

Soph. You !—no, indeed :——

En. Why, then, I muft tell you, that you are a little confident, felf-fufficient minx, and not the perfon I took you for.—But pray, young woman, what is your name ?

Soph. Flora, fir, Don Guzman's daughter. I have left my father's houfe in purfuit of my lover ; who, as yet, knows nothing of the matter.

En. Hum !—this may turn to my advantage ;— for Sophia I know, is fond of Octavio, and, if fhe fhould be jealous of Flora, fhe will then confent to marry me, in revenge for Octavio's falfehood. { *Afide.* } ——Well, mifs, to fhew you my good-nature, I'll forgive the affront you offered me ; I will endeavour to find you a lover, and fend him to you immediately.—In the mean time, here comes a friend of mine I can confide in: he will take care of you while I look for Octavio.

Enter LORENZO.

Es. Lorenzo, this is a young lady, whofe lover I am going in fearch of: you will take her to my lodgings, 'till I find him.—Be fure take particular care of her.

Soph. Oh, fir, now that you are acquainted with my fituation, fure you won't deceive me ;—if you do, it will render me miferable !——

Lor. Well faid, female politician.

A I R.

Lor.　*Had I a heart for falfehood fram'd,*
　　　　　I ne'er could injure you :
　　　　For, tho' your tongue no promife claim'd,
　　　　　Your charms would make me true.

　　　　To you no foul fhall bear deceit,
　　　　　Nor ftranger offer wrong;
　　　　For friends in all the ag'd you'll meet,
　　　　　And brothers in the young.

　　　　But when they learn that you have bleft,
　　　　　Another with your heart,
　　　　They'll bid afpiring paffions reft,
　　　　　And act a brother's part.

　　　　Then, lady, dread not here deceit,
　　　　　Nor fear to fuffer wrong ;
　　　　For friends in all the ag'd you'll meet,
　　　　　And brothers in the young.

DIALOGUE.

Enoch. My mistress expects me, and I must go to her,
Or how can I hope for a smile ?
Louisa. Soon may you return a prosperous wooer ;
But think what I suffer the while !
Alone and away from the man that I love,
In strangers I'm forc'd to confide.
Enoch. Dear lady, my friend you may trust, and he'll
prove
Your servant, protector, and guide.

AIR.

Lor.   Gentle maid, ah ! why suspect me ?
Let me serve thee——then reject me.
Can'st thou trust—and I deceive thee ?
Art thou sad——and shall I grieve thee ?
Gentle maid, ah ! why suspect me ?
Let me serve thee——then reject me.

TRIO.

Louisa. Never may'st thou happy be
If in aught thou'rt false to me !
Lor.   Never may I happy, &c.
Enoch. Never may he, &c.

En. I am sure my good friend will do all in his power to amuse you, 'till I find Octavio, and send him to you—I must on another errand.

ACT II. SCENE I.

Parlour in Don Pedro's House. Enter DON PEDRO
and ENOCH, *meeting.*

Don Pedro.

AH ! little Enoch, I rejoice to see thee,——I have
been——thinking of thee, and have been planning for
your happiness.

En. Don Pedro, you are too good to me; and I
am much obliged to you—I dare say you have thought
me tardy in my visit : but a circumstance has detain-
ed me which I will inform you of.—Your neighbour,
Don Guzman's daughter, is run away from her fa-
ther :— I met her in my way hither, and she sent me
to seek Octavio.——You see I can keep a secret.

D. Ped. Ah, Enoch, see when my daughter will
serve me such a trick.—I am wiser than them all. —I
have locked her up, to make sure of her.

En. And see when my mistress will serve me so.—
My aunt always called me wife little Solomon ; let
Enoch alone ; he's a cunning little dog ; a little
roguish, now and then, in money matters ; but keen,
devilish keen !—I will send Octavio to her ; in which
case he will be no longer my rival with Sophia !—
Ay, ay ! I am devilish keen.—But, what hopes of suc-
cess have I with your fair daughter ?

D. Ped. Why, indeed, fhe is like all her fex—a lit-
tle perverfe :—but, I have lock'd her up, and have
fworn never to fee her more, 'till fhe is obedient to
my commands ;—and, to-morrow, Enoch, I intend
you fhall marry her.—Oh! fhe is a beautiful crea-
ture.

En. I do not doubt it—Pleafe, fir, to give me a de-
fcription of her.

D. Ped. With all my heart.—Let me fee now.—
Her eyes are like diamonds of the firft water ;——

En. Diamonds of the firft water ; that's very good :
But I had much rather they were real diamonds.

[Afide.

D. Ped. Her fkin is like the pureft dimity ;—her
teeth are even, and whiter and better enamelled than
elephant's—and her voice is like a Virginian nightin-
gale's;——and, as for dimples—hold, hold ; dimples
did I fay ?—No, fhe has but one dimple ; but I defy
you to tell which is the prettieft, the cheek that has
the dimple, or, the cheek that has not the dimple :—
then, her chin ;—fhe has a lovely down on her chin,
like the down of a peach.

En. Lord! Lord! I am afraid I fhall be overpow-
ered with her beauty ; and I fhould not care to be in
love with any thing but her money :—but, for my
part, I don't much mind whether handfome or other-
wife.—

A I R.

*En. Give Enoch the nymph who no beauty can boaft,
    But health and good-humour to make her his toaft;*

B

If straight, I don't mind whether slender or fat,
At six feet, or four—we'll ne'er quarrel for that.

Whate'er her complexion, I vow I don't care ;
If brown it is lasting—more pleasing if fair :
And, tho' in her cheeks I no dimples should see,
Let her smile—and each dell is a dimple to me.

Let her locks be the reddest that ever were seen,
And her eyes—may be e'en any colour but green ;
For in eyes, tho' so various the lustre and hue,
I swear I've no choice——only let her have two.

'Tis true I'd dispense with a throne on her back,
And, white teeth I own—are genteeler than black,
A little round chin too's a beauty I've heard,
But I only desire——that she mayn't have a beard.

D. Ped. There ! there ! go your ways to her : that
way leads to her chamber ;——the maid will conduct
you to the apartment.

En. I must confess, I feel a little bashful.—— How
should I address her ;--Do you think she will be struck
with my figure ?

D. Ped. You a lover !—and ask that question—let
me instruct you——

AIR.

D. Ped.   *When the maid whom we love,*
No intreaties can move,

Who'd lead a life of pining ?
If her charms will excuse
The fond rashness you use,
—Away with idle whining !
Ne'er stand like a fool,
With looks sheepish and cool ;—
Such bashful love is teazing ;
But with spirit address,
And, you're sure of success ;
For honest warmth is pleasing.

Nay, tho' wedlock's in view,
Like a rake if you'll woo,
Girls sooner quit their coldness :
They know beauty inspires,
Less respect than desires————
Hence love is prov'd by boldness.————
So ne'er stand like a fool, &c.

[*Exit* Don Pedro.

SCENE II.

Chamber.—Enter ENOCH.

En. Hark ! I thought I heard her !—No ; it was
only my fears !—Lord ! she must be a most beautiful
and enchanting creature !—I think I hear the rat-
tling of silks :—it must be she:—O, here she comes.

B 2

Enter GOVERNESS, *dreſſed like* Sophia.

Gov. Sir, your ſervant—

En. Your ſervant, madam—

Gov. My papa has informed me, ſir, that you are the gentleman has kindly profeſſed a partiality for me—— Will you pleaſe to ſit down, ſir?

En. Madam, I hope—I hópe, madam. [*Advances ſlowly towards the chair.*] O law!—[Governeſs advancing to the chair.] I don't know what to ſay.— [*Sees her.*] Zounds! what a witch!——

Gov. What's the matter, ſir?—you appear frighten'd.

En. No, madam, I'm oblig'd to you.—Zounds! is this the bit of dimity he told me of?—But as long as ſhe has money enough, I'll try to reconcile her looks. [*Aſide.*

Gov. I hope you are not ill, ſir?——

En. Only a little ſurpriz'd, madam :—your beauty has overcome me.—Yes, ſhe has the down upon her chin ſure enough. [*Aſide.*]

Gov. Do, pray ſit down, ſir :—you'll wonder at my condeſcenſion, ſir ;—but I was informed you was the pooreſt little diminutive wretch ;—that you was ill-made, yellow-faced, ſnub-nos'd ;—inſtead of which, I find you ſo genteel, ſo well bred, that I proteſt I am quite charm'd with you——

En. There is ſomething very pretty in the tone of her voice.

Gov. You are really fo captivating, that I am quite delighted with you—fo much, that maiden modefty gives way to the ftriking proportion of your perfon—

En. Faith, now I look at her again, fhe is not quite fo ugly. [*Drawing nearer.*] Will you pardon me, madam, if I falute you. [*Kiffes her.*] Faugh!—a man might as well kifs a hedge-hog. [*Afide.*]

Gov. But, fir, you muft pardon me—you fhould get rid of that filthy beard :—I proteft it is like an artichoke. ——

En. Why, as you fay, mifs, the razor would not be amifs—for either of us. [*Afide.*]—But, I am told you have a fweet voice, mifs—will you pleafe to favour me with a fong—by way of paffing the time?

Gov. My papa, fir, is afraid to truft me even with my mufic-mafter; and I have not practifed for fome time :—But, I'll try. [*Endeavouring to fing but screams.*]

En. Very like a Virginian nightingale! [*Afide.*]

Gov. I'm very hoarfe, fir.

En. Oh, pray, mifs, don't trouble yourfelf to fing any more : I hear you are very hoarfe :—but, perhaps, if you took it lower, it would not oblige you to make fuch very wry faces.

Gov. I have a very great cold, fir ;—but to pleafe fo accomplifhed a gentleman, I'll endeavour to recollect my laft new words.

A I R.

Gov.   *When a tender maid*
            Is firft effay'd

By some admiring swain,
How her blushes rise,
If she meets his eyes,
While he unfolds his pain !
If he takes her hand—she trembles quite !
Touch her lips—and she swoons outright,
While a pit-a-pat, &c.
Her heart avows her fright.

But in time appear
Fewer signs of fear :
The youth she boldly views :
If her hand he grasp,
Or her bosom clasp,
No mantling blush ensues !
Then to church well pleased the lovers move,
While her smiles her contentment prove ;
And a pit-a-pat, &c.
Her heart avows her love !

En. Well, Miss Sophia, may I hope for the happiness of calling you mine, to-morrow ?---It is your father's desire, and what I most ardently wish for.---

Gov. One thing promised, and I shall freely consent.---As my father treated me with such severity, I made a vow never to receive a husband from his hands : but, if you will obtain the key of the garden gate, under pretence of our walking, I will elope from thence with you.

En. [*Pausing.*] In that case, I shall not be obliged to make any settlement on her. [*Aside.*]---Yes, miss, I will endeavour to prevail upon your father ; as I am very much in his good graces.

Enter LORENZO.

Lor. Well faid, brother Enoch, that is to be :—I
fee you are a brifk, and I hope a thriving wooer.

En. As to that, thriving enough ;—but, as to your
fifter, pray was you ever told there was a family like-
nefs ?

Gov. What does my brother fay, Mr. Enoch ?

En. I am fo puzzled, I don't know what to fay.—
Do, for heaven's fake, fay or fing fomething to pleafe
her.

Lor. I'd ftrive to pleafe you both.—She is very te-
nacious of her beauty.—

En. I don't doubt it :—fhe has a damn'd deal of it;
and fhe ought to hold it faft.

A I R.

Lor. *Ah, fure a pair was never feen,*
  So juftly form'd to meet by nature !
The youth excelling fo in mien,
  The maid in ev'ry grace of feature !
O, how happy are fuch lovers,
When kindred beauties each difcovers !
    For furely fhe
    Was made for thee,
And thou to blefs this lovely creature !

So mild your looks, your children thence,
Will early learn the tafk of duty,

The boys with all their father's sense,
  The girls with all their mother's beauty ;
O, how happy to inherit,
At once such graces and such spirit !
    Thus while you live,
    May Fortune give——
Each blessing——equal to your merit !

En. Lorenzo, I thank thee.   Now, miss, I'll wait
upon your father and obtain the key.

Gov. Besure you don't tell my papa how complying
I have been.

En. O, you may depend, miss, upon my prudence.
Such a damn'd piece of conceit and ugliness I never saw
in my life. [*Aside.*]   [*Exeunt severally.*

Enter DON PEDRO *and* ENOCH.

D. Ped. Well, Enoch, what reception did you meet
with ?—Is not she a fine girl ?—She has her grandfa-
ther's lip to a hair.

En. And her grandfather's chin to a hair. [*Aside.*]

D. Ped. Well, Enoch, what reception did you meet
with ? How did my daughter behave ?

En. Why, better than I thought :—But pray, how
old may your daughter be ?

D. Ped. Let me see :—twelve and eight—ay—is just
twenty.

En. Then I'll venture to say, she is the oldest look-
ing girl of her age in the kingdom.—Why, zounds !

she might pass for my grandmother:—and as to her skin, that you told me was like the purest dimity, by this light it is downright nankeen:—And then, her teeth being white—why, they're as black as a coal; where one is ivory its neighbour is pure ebony, alternately black and white like the keys of an harpsichord:—Her voice, too, you told me, was like a Virginian nightingale: why, it's like a crack'd warming pan:—And, as for dimples!—To be sure she has the devil's own dimples!—Yes! and you told me she had a lovely down upon her chin, like the down of a peach;—but, damme, if ever I saw such down upon any human creature in my life, except once upon an old goat.

D. Ped. What, sir! do you mean to insult me, and abuse my daughter, that is allowed to be the handsomest girl in all Spain!—But, I suppose you want to be off from the match.

En. What the devil shall I say now?—Why then, seriously, Don Pedro, do you think your daughter handsome?

D. Ped. The finest girl in all Spain!——

En. Lord! Lord! How partial some parents are to their children!—Then, since you provoke me to speak, she's a downright witch——

Enter LORENZO.

Lor. Hey day!—you seem to be upon odd terms, for a father and son-in-law.

D. Ped. What's that to you, you jack-a-napes!

En. He looks plaguy angry with me, I believe I had
better draw in my horns, or I shan't have his bit of
dimity. [*Aside.*]

AIR.

Enoch.   *Believe me, good fir, I ne'er meant to offend ;*
My miftrefs I love, and I value my friend :
To win her and wed her, is ftill my requeft,
For better for worfe—and I fwear I don't jeft.

D. Ped.   *Zounds ! you'd beft not provoke me my rage is*
fo high.

Enoch.   *Hold him faft I befeech you, his rage is fo high.*
Good fir you're too hot, and this place I muft fly.

D. Ped.   *You're a knave and a fot, and this place had*
beft fly.

En. You are in fuch a paffion now :---[*Going to
him.*]---Did you think I was in earneft ?--I was but
jefting all the while.---You're fo hafty, Don Pedro ;
I had only a mind to joke a little ; that was all, upon
my honour !

D. Ped. Then you was not in earneft ?---Zounds !
I thought you were in earneft.---But, I can forgive a
joke as well as any one :---but take care how you carry
your jokes fo far ; for I was near being in a bit of a
paffion. Come, get fome wine here ; and that will
drown all animofities.

AIR——TRIO.

Don Pedro, Enoch, and Lorenzo.

A bumper of good liquor,
Will end a contest quicker,
Than justice, judge, or vicar :
So fill a chearful glass,
And let good humour pass.

But if more deep the quarrel,
Why sooner drain the barrel,
Than be the hateful fellow,
That's crabbed when he's mellow.
A bumper, &c.

SCENE IV.

---

*Street:---*ENOCH *and* OCTAVIO, *meeting.*

En. Good day, Octavio :---I am glad to have met
you : I have been in pursuit of you.

Oct. I am happy you have found me. What is your
business with me, Enoch ?

En. Only a little love affair :---that's all.---Flora is
run away from her father, Don Guzman ; and has

laid her commands upon me, to bring you to her.—
You have no objection, I hope, fir :—a very fine
girl !

Oa. Two things forbid it : friendfhip and honour.
Flora, Don Guzman's daughter !—It cannot be me
fhe fent for.

En. Oh, damn your friendfhip and honour.—Go
to her. I fay it was you fhe fent for, and go you
muft. She is all impatience, and waiting at Don Lo-
renzo's lodgings.—Come, come, and I'll conduct you
to her.

Oa. Well, I'll go to her.—Poffibly I may be able to
erve her, with regard to my friend Lorenzo. [*Afide.*]
Lead on Enoch, and I'll follow.

En. Methinks you are devilifh loath to vifit a pretty
wench.—If fhe had fent for me, I fhould have taken
pity on her inftantly.   [*Exeunt.*

SCENE V.

Enter Sophia.

A I R.

What bard, O Time, difcover,
 With wings firft made thee move !
Ah ! fure he has fome lover
 Who ne'er had left his love !

For, who that once did prove
The pangs which absence brings,
 Tho' but one day,
 He were away,
Could picture thee with wings ?
What bard, &c.

Enter LORENZO.

Soph. What has detained you fo long ?—Where is Octavio, dear brother ?

Lor. I have been in fearch of him, but, without fuccefs : Enoch is now in purfuit of him.

Soph. Cruel, cruel man !—You was never in love ; elfe you would not fport with the anxiety of a tender heart ! [Lorenzo *fighs.*] But, was you, Lorenzo, was you ever in love ?—

Lor. I was, Sophia.

Soph. And, was your miftrefs true ?

Lor. Oh ! had fhe been always fo I had been happy.

A I R.

Lor. *Oh, had my love ne'er fmil'd on me,*
  I ne'er had known fuch anguifh,
 But, think how falfe, how cruel fhe,
  To bid me ceafe to languifh ;
 To bid me hope her hand to gain,
  Breathe on a flame half perifh'd,
 And then, with cold and fix'd difdain,
  To kill the hope fhe cherifh'd !

Not worse his fate—who, on a wreck
That drove as winds did blow it—
Silent had left the shatter'd deck
To find a grave below it :
Then land was cried—no more resign'd,.
He glow'd with joy to hear it,
—Not worse his fate—his woe to find.
The wreck must sink e'er near it.

Enter a SERVANT.

Ser. Two gentlemen below, fir.
Soph. Octavio and Enoch, no doubt. We'll retire
a moment, to fee Octavio's furprize. Let us ftep in-
to this room.   [*Goes to the door of the scene.*

Enter OCTAVIO, ENOCH, *and* SERVANT.

En. Where is Flora ?—I have found Octavio, and
have brought him to you at laft : for it was with great
difficulty I perfuaded him to come with me. [*Servant*
points to the door where Sophia *is.—*Octavio *goes in re-*
luctantly.]
En. I think I'll juft take a peep, to fee the meeting.
So, fo, I think he has pretty well reconciled his friend-
fhip and honour to the interview.—He does not feem
to feel any qualms of confcience now. I'll leave
them to fettle the reft, and purfue my own bufinefs.
                                                [*Exit.*

Enter Sophia, Octavio, *and* Lorenzo.

Oct. And are you fure the Jew does not fufpect the plot contrived againft him?

Soph. Not in the leaft. He is too vain of his own perfon; and money is his aim: therefore he thinks every charm is centered in Urfula.

Oct. How fhall I thank you, my dear Sophia! for the confidence you repofe in me?—Alas! I feared my all was loft; confidering my want of fortune, and that your father's cruelty would oblige us to renounce our love.

Lor. Permit me, my dear friend, to wifh you joy on this happy meeting.——May every hour of your life prove as happy as the prefent!

Oct. I thank you, my dear Lorenzo.—And now, Sophia, that happinefs is within our reach, why fhould we delay one moment?——I'll go and bring a prieft, that fhall put it out of the power of man to part us.

[*Going.*

Soph. [*Stopping him.*] Stay, Octavio!—Though I have been fo imprudent as to leave my father's houfe, and fly to you for protection, it was to avoid the hated marriage with the Jew:—But you'll fhew your love by leaving the management of this to my direction.

Lor. Come, come, Octavio, as my fifter has hitherto confided in you, 'tis but juft you fhould let her now command.

Oct. I muft obey.——But, why do we trifle with

the hours, fo precious to us both ?——Your father muft be reconciled, when we are made one.

Soph. No more, I befeech you.——I will go to my friend Flora's apartment, and write my letter. I hope you will not fail to meet me there.

Oct. I fubmit with pleafure and fhall be impatient for the moment.

A I R.——Trio.

Octavio, Lorenzo, *and* Sophia.

Soft pity never leaves the gentle breaft,
Where love has been receiv'd a welcome gueft ;
As wand'ring faints poor huts have facred made,
He hallows ev'ry heart he once has fway'd ;
And (when his prefence we no longer fhare),
Still leaves compaffion as a relic there.

ACT III. SCENE I.

Hall in Don Pedro's *House.—Enter* DON PEDRO *and*
SERVANT.

Don Ped o.

WELL, to be sure ; thefe women are ftrange beings.:
they never know their own minds a minute.——Why
now, it was but this morning, that fhe could never
marry Enoch, becaufe he was a Jew : and behold
this afternoon, fhe is eloped with him.——Are you
fure it was them ?——

Serv. O yes, fir, it was indeed. I faw them in a
poft-chaife, driving from the garden gate. You
know, fir, it was by your commands the gardener
gave him the key to walk with my young lady on the
parterre.

D. Ped. I rejoice to hear it ;—the news makes my
old heart glad ;—and my daughter will be happy.

Enter SERVANT, *with a letter.*

Serv. My mafter, Enoch, fends this letter with all
due refpect to your honour.

D. Ped. Here, give it me, you dog.—This is to
inform me, I fuppofe, he is married, and to crave

my leave to return.—I am tranfported !—[*Reads.*]
" *Sir, your approbation of what I have already done*
" *would give me the greateft pleafure : I am anxious to*
" *receive your blefng, and will immediately return, if*
" *I have your permiffion. Sophia's duty to her deareft*
" *father. By the time this reaches your hand I fhall be*
" *honoured with the title of your fon-in-law.*

Enoch Iffachar."

——As I could wifh !——Here, Lopez ! Francis
Vafquez ! put on your beft liveries ; throw open all
the doors ; call the cook ; bid him prepare a fupper
with all the delicacies Spain affords :——bid all my
neighbours welcome ; and requeft them to partake
my happinefs ; tell them I expeft my fon and daugh-
ter home.——Get the keys of the cellar, and make
all happy.

Enter fecond SERVANT, *with a letter.*

Serv. This from my young miftrefs.

D. Ped. Why, ay, this is from Sophia.——Since
Enoch wrote to me, what needs the little baggage trou-
ble herfelf ?—One would think they were not toge-
ther when thefe were wrote.—Let me fee—[*Reads.*]
" *Deareft papa, tho' I have been fo imprudent as to*
" *leave your houfe, I hope you will pardon the indifcre-*
" *tion : It is with a man who is paffionately fond of me,*
" *and whofe merits equally claim my regard. Your con-*
" *fent, before the ceremony is performed, will make*
" *bleffed your dutiful daughter,   Sophia.*"

Go, get pen, ink, and paper in my room, that I

may send my consent with all haste.——My heart is
so light, methinks I have renewed my age.

AIR.

D. Ped. *O the days when I was young,*
         When I laugh'd in fortune's spight,
         Talk'd of love the whole day long,
         And with nectar crown'd the night.

         Then it was, old father Care,
         Little reck'd I of thy ffrown;
         Half thy malice youth could bear,
         And the rest a bumper drown.
                 O the days, &c.

         Truth they say lies in a well;
         Why I vow I ne'er could see——
         Let the water-drinkers tell,
                 ——There it always lay for me :

         For, when sparkling wine went round,
         Never saw I falsehood's mask :
         But still honest truth I found
                 ——In the bottom of each flask.
                 O the days, &c.

         True, at length my vigour's flown,
         I have years to bring decay ;
         Few the locks that now I own,
         And the few I have are grey :

Yet old Jerome thou may'ft boaft,
While the fpirits do not tire,
Still beneath thy age's froft
Glows a fpark of youthful fire.
O the days, &c.

SCENE II.

Street.—Enter LORENZO, *walking about uneafy.*

Lor. To what a dreadful dilemma have I brought
myfelf by my own fond officious folly!—to lofe the
only object upon earth I could be happy with!—Yet,
why fhould I condemn myfelf?—It is too plain her af-
fections are eftranged; and Octavio is the happy man.

A I R.

Lor. Ah! cruel maid, how haft thou chang'd
The temper of my mind!
My heart, by thee from mirth eftrang'd,
Becomes like thee unkind!

By fortune favour'd, clear in fame,
I once ambitious was;
And friends I had that fann'd the flame,
And gave my youth applaufe.——

But now my weaknefs all abuse,
  Yet vain their taunts on me,
Friends, fortune, fame itfelf, I'd lofe,
  To gain one fmile from thee !

Yet only thou fhouldft not defpife
  My folly or my woe ;
If I am mad in others eyes,
  'Tis thou haft made me fo.

But days like thefe with doubting curft
  I will not long endure :
Am I defpis'd ?—I know the worft,
  And alfo know my cure.

If falfe, her vows fhe dare renounce,
  She inftant ends my pain :
For, oh ! that heart muft break at once
  —Which cannot hate again !

Enter ENOCH, *haftily.*

Lor. Whither in fuch hafte, Enoch ?—What's the matter ?

En. O, Lorenzo, is that you ?—What think you of the gentle Flora, Don Guzman's daughter ?—She is run away from her father, for the fake of her lover, and fhe fays he knows nothing of the matter.

Lor. Dear girl ! no more I did.—Where is fhe?

En. Be but patient, and I'll tell you all.—She fent for him.———

Lor. Well, carry me to her this moment! [*Dragging* Enoch.] Carry me to her!

En. Well, well, mercy on us, how violent you are! --Why I did carry the person she sent for : It was Don Octavio.

Lor. Octavio, that she sent for!

En. Yes it was.——But he was devilish loth to go, 'till I perfuaded him.——He talked much about friendship and honour.——but I faid, damn your honour.

Lor. The devil, you did.——Oh! wretch that I am! mifery and diftraction come upon me!

En. Why, fure you was not the fool that was in love with her.—— Ha! ha! ha!

Lor. You unfeeling Ifraelite!——you dog! don't you pity me? [*Collaring him.*

En. O, yes, fir, I do pity you moft heartily. Dear brother in law!——

Lor. You do pity me, do you, villain?
[*Going to beat him.*

En. O, no, fir, upon my foul, I do not pity you: my dear brother-in-law!

Lor. There, then :——take that villain! and that ——and that. [*Following him round the ftage beating him.*]

En. Oh! my dear brother-in-law—that is to be— Oh! fpare me, my dear brother!——

Lor. Then, firrah, begone! and remember, 'tis only your infignificance that protects you.

En. Then, egad my infignificance is the beft friend I ever had in all my life.——Oh! what a curfed, bully-headed, bloody-minded, fwaggering dog it is!
[*Exit, ftealing off.*

A I R.

Lor. *Sharp is the woe that wounds the jealous mind,*
When treach'ry two fond hearts would rend!
But oh! how keener far the pang, to find
That traitor in our bosom friend!

SCENE III.

A Wood.—Enter Flora, Sophia, *and* Octavio.

A I R.

Flo. *By him we love offended,*
How soon our anger flies!
One day apart 'tis ended,
Behold him, and it dies!

Last night your roving brother
Enrag'd I bade depart,
And sure his rude presumption
Deserv'd to lose my heart :—
Yet, were he now before me,
In spight of injur'd pride,
I fear my eyes would pardon—
Before my tongue could chide.
By him we love, &c.

With truth the bold deceiver
  To me thus oft has said——
' *In vain would Flora slight me,*
  ' *In vain she would upbraid!* '
' *No scorn those lips discover——*
  ' *Where dimples laugh the while ;*
' *No frowns appear resentful,*
  ' *Where heav'n has stamp'd a smile !*'
  By him we love, &c.

Flo. My dear Sophia, you will foon be happy.——
For my part, I am doom'd to pafs the long folitary
hours in this dreary manfion---Heigho.   [*Sighing.*
  Soph. Indeed, my dear, you are miftaken : for, if
my father does not give his confent, how are we to
live ?—without a fortune, without friends of courfe—
  Oct. Do not grieve, my deareft love ?——

A I R.

Oct.   *How oft, Louifa, haft thou faid*
       (Nor wilt thou the fond boaft difown)
    Thou wouldft not lofe Octavio, love !
       To reign the partner of a throne !

    And by thofe lips that fpoke fo kind !
       And by this hand I prefs'd to mine !
    —To gain a fubject nation's love,
       I fwear I would not part with thine.

Then how my foul, can we be poor,
　Who own what kingdoms could not buy !
Of this true heart thou fhalt be queen,
　And, ferving thee—a monarch I.

Thus, uncontroul'd in mutual blifs,
　And rich in love's exhauftlefs mine—
Do thou fnatch treafures from my lips,
　And I'll take kingdoms back from thine !

Enter a Nun, *veiled, with a letter.*

Soph. Now, indeed, we are nearer happinefs. Here's
a wonderful change ;---my father's free confent.

Oĉt. Is it poffible !--This is joy beyond expreffion!
---Let us no longer delay our blifs !---I will fly and
bring the prieft.

Soph. Stay, Octavio.

Oĉt. My life !————

Soph. Had not you better take me with you ?--per-
haps you will not find me here on your return.

Oĉt. Thus let me thank thee for thy fond advice.
[*Kiffes her.*]　　　　　[*Exeunt Oĉt. and Soph.*

Flo. There they go, as happy as heart can wifh :--
May every bleffing attend them !

Enter Lorenzo, *looking after* Octavio *and* Sophia.

Flo. So ! this fhould be Lorenzo.—How got he in,
I wonder ?—By the help of a bribe, no doubt.

Lor. [*Looking after them.*] There is Octavio with

C

her; and, for aught I know, going to be married.——
I shall run diſtracted!   [Going.

   Flo. Sir, ſir!   [*Stopping him.*

   Lor. Pſha! let me alone.——

   Flo. What do you want, ſir?—you appear unhap-
py.

   Lor. Not you, child, not you.—But, pray, good
nun, is not that Octavio?

   Flo. Aſſuredly it is.

   Lor. And is not that Flora with him?

   Flo. Flora is not yet gone out of the garden.

   Lor. One queſtion more; and I'll trouble you no
further.—Are they going to be married?

   Flo. They are, ſir.

   Lor. Oh! unfortunate that I am—But I will fol-
low them——upbraid them with their falſehood——
and—have done for ever.   [*Exit* Lor.

   Flo. Well, I'll follow. Sophia may not be the
only bride to-day.

AIR.

  Flo. *Adieu, thou dreary pile, where never dies*
    The ſullen echo of repentant ſighs!
    Ye ſiſter mourners of each lonely cell,
    Inur'd by hymns and ſorrow, fare you well!
    For happier ſcenes, I fly this darkſome grove,
    ——To ſaints a priſon, but a tomb to love!

SCENE IV.

Monastery —Enter Father John, *Father* Titus, *Father* Matthew, *and other Friars, drinking.*

GLEE and CHORUS.

This bottle's the sun of our table,
His beams are rosy wine,
We——planets who are not able,
Without his help to shine.

Let mirth and glee abound,
You'll soon grow bright,
With borrowed light,
And shine as he goes round!

F. John. Come, fill.   Here's to the blue-ey'd nun
of St. Catharine's.   [*Drinks.*

All. Agreed.—The blue-ey'd nun of St. Catha-
rine's.   [*Drinks.*

F. John. Here's to the mother abbess.   [*Drinks.*

All. To our mother abbess.   [*Drinks.*

F. John. Have there been any legacies or donations
since our last meeting?

F. Matt. Fifty pounds from an usurer, on his death-
bed, to pray his soul through purgatory.

F. John. Well, that will pay for our candles, bro-
ther Matthew. Any thing more?

C 2

F. Matt. A thousand dollars, from a lady, to be applied to charitable uses.

F. John. The best of uses——to discharge our wine bill.

F. Matt. A large silver lamp, by Don Emanuel de Castro, to be kept continually burning in the tomb of St. Anthony.

F. John. Which we will melt down, to bring in more luscious provisions, than any we have yet mentioned ; for St. Anthony is not afraid to be left in the dark—tho' he was——

F. Matt. Forty pistoles I have received for confession.

F. John. Very good——that will help to pay our butcher's bill.

> [*A loud knocking at the door ;—they all
> retire, but* John *and* Matthew.

Enter a PORTER, *meagre and pale.*

F. John. [*With a glass in his hand.*] What dost thou want ?

Porter. I thought you had done your morning rites.

F. John. Done !—No !—Have we, brother Matthew ?

F. Matt. No, not by a bottle, man.

F. John. I suppose thy sinful disposition has brought thee to see what was to be had to gratify thy worldly voracious appetite. Thy pamper'd looks are a scandal to our order.—If you are hungry, are there not the roots of the earth ?—[*Eats cake.*]—And, if you are dry, is there not the clear stream ?—[*Drinks wine.*]

Porter. Some company would fpeak with your holi-
nefs, if your morning devotions are ended.

      [*Father* John *drinks, and gives the glafs*
          to the Porter, *who puts it to his mouth.*

F. John. So, you finful wretch, if there had been
any thing in it, you would have drank it.—Admit.
them.

SCENE V.

Enter Octavio *and* Enoch.

Oct. We are come, father, to folicit your aid, to
join us in nuptial bands, and hope not too late.

F. John. Yes, fir, but you are, by half an hour ;—
you muft be patient, and wait another day.

Oct. But, good father, love is impatient, and we
cannot wait ;—pray, difpatch us. [*Giving gold.*] And
let this plead for me.

F. John. Nay, now you offended me grofsly —I
muft not take gold ; it hurts my confcience :—but,
here's a place in my habit, you may lodge it in : – up-
on your own head be the fin.——And on this fide is
another. ——

En. O, I underftand you.—There, father.—I
fhall need your help prefently ; but difpatch your pre-
fent office.

F. John. The fins of this town almoft diftract me—

they make me linger in flesh to see them daily commit-
ted before my eyes.

Oct. One would imagine, indeed, they were under
your nose ; for it blushes more than the rest of your
face.

En. Here comes Lorenzo : I'll not stay, for he's
a desperate fellow —Octavio, you had better go.

Oct. Why should I fear him ?—Blessed with my
love, I'll stand my ground.

En. The devil take me if I do ;—he almost broke
my bones just now ; so I'll take my leave.—Father,
you shall see me again.   ◢   [*Exit.*

Enter LORENZO.

Lor. Octavio, is this your friendship ?—How can
you answer for such treatment ?—Thy life shall pay
for it :—Draw, sir !   [*Draws.*

Soph. Why, brother, you appear angry : [*Disco-
vering herself*] What's the matter ?

Enter FLORA *behind him, veiled.*

F. John. Certainly the man has not a mind to marry
his own sister.

Lor. Sophia !—Is it you that I have mistaken for
Flora all this while ?—Where is she fled ?

Flo. What is it you want, sir——Not you, child,
not you——   [*Mocking him.*

Oct. Octavio, I blush for my folly—Sophia, what
shall I say ?—Flora, my angel, can you forgive me ?
Love is blind.

DUETTO.

Oft does Hymen smile to hear,
Worldly vows of feign'd regard ;
Well he knows when they're sincere,
Never slow to give reward.

For his glory is to prove
Kind to those who wed for love.

SCENE VI.

Enter DON PEDRO.

D. Ped. Methinks they are very flow :—I wish they were come.—Oh, here's Enoch.

Enter ENOCH.

En. I am returned with joy to crave your blessing.

D. Ped. But where's my daughter !—my dear girl !—Why did not she accompany you ?—Every moment is an age, 'till I see her.

En. She is waiting for your permission to throw herself at your feet.

D. Ped. Run !—Bring her to me !—She'll gladden my old heart.   [*Exit* Enoch.]—I am all joy.

Enter Enoch *and* Governess.

D. Ped. O Lord!—Is that my daughter?—Why the man is surely mad!

En. Why do you look at her fo, fir?—Go, my dear, and throw your fnowy arms round your papa.—He will forgive you. Don't be fo uneafy—go to him—

Gov. My dear papa! [*Running to bim and embracing bim.*] You will not fure be fo cruel as to difown me!

D. Ped. Papa! dear papa!—What the devil do you mean, you have not married Urfula, the old Governefs, have you, inftead of my beautiful daughter?

Gov. O, you are a cruel parent!

D. Ped. O Lord! Lord! will nobody relieve me from this old hag.

En. Did I not tell you, fhe was as ugly as the devil; and you would not believe me?—And fo, then, I am taken in with this old Jezzabel.

Gov. I'll let you know whether I am not a match too good for you.

Enter Octavio *and* Sophia.

Oct. I am come, fir, with my dear Sophia, to afk forgivenefs, and to claim your blefling.

D. Ped. You fhall have neither, fir!—You have cheated me of my daughter;—and do you think I can fo eafily forgive it?

Oct. There, fir, is your own confent, in your hand-writing, figned by your own name.

D. Ped. Sir, it was through a ſtratagem you obtain-
ed that conſent :—and you ſhall not poſſeſs a rial of
her fortune.

Soph. Believe me, ſir, I never meant to deceive
you, to marry without your conſent.—I would not
receive Octavio for a huſband, until I obtained it by
your letter.

D. Ped. No matter, madam.—You ſhall not have a
marvedie of your fortune.

Oſt. I care not, ſir.—In herſelf I have a treaſure.—
Give me but your bleſſing, make me happy—and I
am content.

D. Ped. A generous fellow, this. [*Aſide.*]   Do
you think, ſir, you are the only man in Spain that can
.do a generous act ?—There, ſir :—ſince my daughter
is your's, her fortune ſhall be alſo :——There's my
bleſſing, too :——and, ſince you are ſo generous to
deſpiſe her fortune, no man in Spain better deſerves
it.   [*They both kneel.*

Soph. Accept our grateful thanks !——

Enter LORENZO *and* FLORA.

D. Ped. Hey day! What have we here !—Have
you been robbing a nunnery ?

Lor. This is Donna Flora, ſir, Don Guzman's
daughter, and my wife, with a good fortune.

D. Ped. Come here, you little ſlut, and kiſs me.—
You young dog, you have made a good choice.——
Bleſs you my children !—And may you ever be as
happy as at preſent.

En. And muſt I ſtand to my bargain with this old
witch.

Gov. Upon my word ! you have no need to complain ; who are you ! [*Following him round the stage.*] I will let you know, sir, I have a brother, an Alguazile, that wears a sword---you ill-looking diminutive wretch.

En. The devil's dam is broke loose, and her whole fury is levelled at me.

Soph. Well, little Enoch, you were always keen, ——devilish keen.——

Lor. Your mother always called you wise little Solomon.

D. Ped. No body could ever put a trick on you :—— Hey ! Enoch !

Lor. Cunning little Enoch !

En. Is there no way to avoid these everlasting tongues ? This door will befriend me :——I'll fly to Jerusalem to get rid of that bit of dimity. [*Exit* En.

Gov. Fly where you will—— I'll follow you.

[*Exit* Gov.

FINALE and CHORUS.

Come now for jest and smiling,
Both old and young beguiling,
          Let us laugh and play, so blithe and gay,
          'Till we banish care away.
Thus crown'd with dance and song,
The hours shall glide along.
          With a heart at ease—merry, merry glees,
          Can never fail to please.

Each bride with blushes glowing,
Our wine as rosy flowing,
          Let us laugh and play, &c.

Then a health to ev'ry friend,
The night's repast shall end,
        With a heart at ease, &c.

Nor while we are so joyous,
Shall anxious care annoy us,
        Let us laugh and play, &c.
For gen'rous guests like these,
Accept the wish to please.
        So we'll laugh and play, all blithe and gay,
        Your smiles drive care away.

A grand Masquerade Scene, with Dances, &c. &c.

F I N I S.

CPSIA information can be obtained at www.ICGtesting.com
Printed in the USA
BVOW04s1021040314

346623BV00013B/357/P

9 781165 539277